James Andrews has worked in a variety of state comprehensive schools during his thirteen years in teaching, much of which has been a gradual unlearning of what he learned at teacher-training college. He has never sought to be anything other than a bog-standard classroom teacher. He lives in Cornwall, alone.

THE BITTER ROOT

Educating the Wayward Scholar

James Andrews

Illustrations by Darren Fletcher

Published in 2010 by Haven Books,
an imprint of Dexter Haven Ltd
Curtain House
134–146 Curtain Road
London
EC2A 3AR

ISBN: 978-1-903660-09-6

A full CIP record for this book is available from the British Library

Cover design and all illustrations Darren Fletcher

Typeset in Calisto by Dexter Haven Associates Ltd, London
Printed and bound in Great Britain by CPI Antony Rowe, Chippenham

to Mum and Dad with love

We want great alteration but we want nothing new. Alteration, modification to suit the times and circumstances; but the great principles ought to be and must be the same.

William Cobbett

Contents

Preface

In the few thousand years since the advent of institutional education many things have changed: the nature of children is not one of them. With such long experience of a thing that has not fundamentally changed, one might be forgiven for assuming modern educational technique to be highly advanced and effective; instead, however, we find basic errors, arising from a failure to understand the behaviour of real – rather than theoretical – children. It is the wayward scholar who is particularly proficient at exploiting these errors, and it is with him that this book is chiefly concerned; for he wields tremendous influence, and great is his capacity for bringing contention into the lives of others.

A note on gender

Here I would be hard pushed to improve on the preamble
to *The Laws of Cricket* (MCC):

> The use, throughout the text, of pronouns indicating the
> male gender is purely for brevity. Except where specifically
> stated otherwise, every provision of the Laws is to be read
> as applying to women and girls equally as to men and boys.

Rebellion

A little rebellion now and then is a good thing.

Thomas Jefferson

What has happened to indiscipline in our schools? One hardly ever hears of a greased piglet being released into a school assembly these days. What has happened to the great and triumphant acts of indiscipline that used to be the backbone of our educational system? Gone, gone, all gone. And with what have they been replaced? Lateness, white trainers, big earrings and the setting off of fire-extinguishers: indiscipline for any school to be ashamed of.

Somewhat perversely, that I have not been entertained by the spectacle of a greased piglet running amok amongst scholars is suggestive of indiscipline in my school not being what it ought; for it is possible there to attain infamy with far less remarkable, but endlessly repeated, villainies. The spent fire-extinguisher and the hackneyed white trainer are evidence of a system that in no way attempts to be foolproof, and he who bears such items wears no richer crown than that of a mundane fool. And of what use, after all, is a mundane fool? He is an embarrassment to his parents, a disappointment to his teacher, and an annoyance to his classmates:

I Must not Flick lead at lee
I Must not Flick lead at lee
I Must not Flick lead at lee
I Must not Flick lead at lee

Where is the sophisticated and intelligent japery that is the mark of an excellent fool? And where is the disciplinary rigour that nurtures him thus?

We grown-ups love to take a dim view of today's children. We delight in reminiscing over some golden age, usually centred on our own childhood, when things were singularly better; a time when the evils that blight today were unheard of, and when a boy received his thick ear with a 'Thank you, Mister.' But did this time ever exist?

Is there anything whereof it may be said, See, this is new?
It hath been already of old time, which was before us.

Ecclesiastes 1:9–10

The truth is that things have remained remarkably constant, as Peter the Hermit, Aristotle, Plato, Socrates and Hesiod are at pains to point out:

The young people of today think of nothing but themselves. They have no reverence for parents or old age.

They are impatient of all restraint. They talk as if they alone knew everything, and what passes for wisdom with us is foolishness with them. As for girls, they are forward, immodest and unwomanly in speech, behaviour and dress.

extract from a sermon by Peter the Hermit, 1274

When I look at the younger generation, I despair of the future of civilisation.

Aristotle, 384–322 BC

What is happening to our young people? They disrespect their elders, they disobey their parents. They ignore the law. They riot in the streets inflamed with wild notions. Their morals are decaying. What is to become of them?

Plato, 427–347 BC

The children now love luxury. They have bad manners, contempt for authority, they show disrespect for their elders and love chatter in place of exercise. Children are now tyrants; not the servants of their households. They no longer rise when elders enter the room. They contradict their parents, chatter before company, gobble up dainties at the table, cross their legs and tyrannise their teachers.

Socrates, 469–399BC

I see no hope for the future of our people if they are dependant on the frivolous youth of today, for certainly all youth are reckless beyond words…When I was young we were taught to be discreet and respectful of elders, but the present youth are exceedingly wise [disrespectful] and impatient of restraint.

Hesiod, eighth century BC

We live in a decaying age. Young people no longer respect their parents. They are rude and impatient. They frequently inhabit taverns and have no self-control.

inscription, 6000-year-old Egyptian tomb, quoted in R. Buckminster Fuller's *I Seem to Be a Verb*

Hardly a glorious unfolding backwards towards a golden age of civilisation. According to our philosophers, wickedness is not peculiar to the present. Nothing has changed in the rebellious nature of children, it seems, for the last three thousand years at least, and it has certainly not changed in the short time that you and I have been alive. As much as you and I might long for it to be otherwise, there is, unfortunately, nothing unusually bad about this generation of children; they remain largely predictable creatures acting in largely predictable ways. Of course many things which affect children have changed, the most damaging of which has been the invention of adolescence – that great swathe of worklessness and deferred responsibility on which so-called developed societies so pride themselves – but the rebellious nature of the young remains constant.

Why else would Mr Parkin, without my blessing, reunite himself with the crisps that I have confiscated from him and placed on my desk?

Once confiscated, my crisps are not my own
Once confiscated, my crisps are not my own
Once confiscated, my crisps are not my own
Once confiscated, my crisps are not my own

And why else would it be that, being to them a new teacher, Mr Dunlop and Mr Desbrough decide to give me incorrect names, when there is so little to be gained and so much to be lost?

My name is not James
My name is not James
My name is not James
My name is not James

my name is not Chris
my name is not Chris
my name is not Chris
my name is not Chris

Rebelliousness, innate rebelliousness, a deep desire to ridicule authority and to waylay the adult who would seek to do the child the terrible injury of plotting his good. Whereas the desire to have one's own way may fluctuate wildly from person to person, it yet remains a universal desire particularly prevalent in prideful youths, where it is fuelled by a ridicule for old age:

And he thinks of growing old as an almost obscene calamity, which for some mysterious reason will never happen to himself. All who have passed the age of thirty are joyless grotesques, endlessly fussing about things of no importance and staying alive without, so far as the child can see, having anything to live for.

George Orwell, *Such, Such Were the Joys*

The child, of course, loves to push the boundaries, challenge authority, and rebel. This is a good thing, since without it there would be no change. Since neither past nor present societies have been perfect, it is logical to consider that in order for improvements to be made, change must occur.

Unthinking respect for authority is the greatest enemy of truth.

Albert Einstein

History has shown us that revolution traditionally comes from the young; therefore, it is both normal and beneficial to society for young people to rebel. Did we not all do it to some extent when we were younger? And yet do we not still consider society to be better off today for our citizenship?

It is the job of the adult and the teacher to channel the rebellion of the child into something slightly more useful than utter anarchy; to help him to be creative and purposeful in his rebellion, and not to destroy institutions that are there for his own benefit. I recently heard this lament of the apparently disenfranchised: 'It's so hard to be creative when you're forced to wear school uniform.' This schoolboy was simply confusing creativity with wanting his own way; a truly creative child would have taken a needle and thread and made creative alterations, or started an underground newspaper lampooning school authority – in other words a pig, and some grease.

The girls could not take off their panama hats because this was not far from the school gates and hatlessness was an offence. Certain departures from the proper set of the hat on the head were overlooked in the case of fourth-form girls and upwards so long as nobody wore their hat at an angle. But there were other subtle variants from the ordinary rule of wearing the brim turned up at the back and down at the front. The five girls, standing very close to each other because of the boys, wore their hats each with a definite difference...Monica wore her panama hat rather higher on her head than normal, perched as if it were too small and as if she knew she looked grotesque in any case...Rose Stanley was famous for sex. Her hat was placed quite unobtrusively on her blond short hair, but she dented the crown on either side...Eunice Gardiner, small, neat, and famous for her spritely gymnastics and glamorous swimming, had the brim of her hat turned up at the front and down at the back...Sandy Stranger wore it turned up all round and as far back on her head as it could possibly go; to assist this, she had attached to her hat a strip of elastic which went under the chin...Jenny Gray...wore her hat with the front brim bent sharply downwards...

Muriel Spark, *The Prime of Miss Jean Brodie*

There is a marked difference between intelligent rebellion and simply wanting one's own way. When, week in, week out, Mr Dorchester asks to go to the toilet, and I, week in, week out, refuse him that privilege, the reason that he whines so is not because he is desperate to make water, but because he wants, and is used to getting, his own way. He wishes to loiter in the corridor with like-minded malingerers, and dwell in that fellowship of miscreants to which all children, regardless of age or inclination, gain automatic membership when they are given, during lesson time, the freedom of the corridor. More than once, evidently with little effect, I have tried to explain to Mr Dorchester the principle of The Graph of Unlikelihood. I use the graph to show him how, contrary to his thinking, the more times he asks to be excused, the less likely it becomes that I will allow him leave to go.

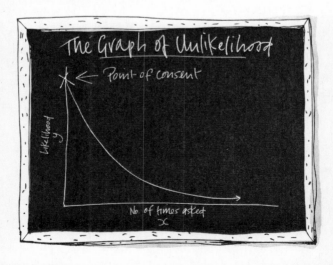

I explain to him that, possibly unlike his parents, I will not be inclined to change my mind in the face of begging, or by the incessant repetition of the words 'please', 'why' and 'not'. I point out to him that he has already fallen well below the point of consent, and that his greatest chance of being allowed to go to the toilet in future lessons is not to ask at all. Miss Whitlock points out that if we extrapolate through the y axis, Mr Dorchester could improve the likelihood of his being excused by asking *not* to go to the toilet – a request to which I would readily assent. Next lesson Mr Dorchester asks not to go to the toilet: he has already become a better kind of fool.

On another occasion Mr Dorchester – pubescent nemesis of mine – accused me of violating his human rights by denying him toilet leave, and demanded justice. By pure and happy coincidence I happened to have a copy of the Universal Declaration of Human Rights to hand – a surprisingly brief document broken down into 30 articles. 'Show me the article that approves your right to go to the toilet during lesson time, Mr Dorchester, and you may go,' quoth I. If he had been given to reading, he would probably have found something to support his claim in Article 13 (1) concerning the right to freedom of movement. But I, quite correctly as it fell out, was banking on the fact that children who want to go to the lavatory on the firm's time, so to speak, are not generally given to studying the black letter.

I have already suggested that many applications for the use of a toilet have nothing to do with any biological need, and are merely a vehicle for achieving undeserved leave. Such was the case of young Mr Stark who, despite his many vociferous petitions, was denied the freedom of the corridor. At the end of the lesson some ten minutes later, and purely for the satisfaction of my curiosity, I followed this same scholar down the corridor, and bless my eyes if he did not walk right past the gentlemen's lavatories with the nonchalance of a chap whose bladder was entirely at ease. Overtaking him, I pointed this out, whereupon he wore a goose look, and offered falteringly that he had a preference for the facilities in another part of the school, to which he now meant to bend his steps. Some weeks later, when Mr Stark had regained a measure of his former audacity, he once again asked to be excused, and I, wishing to foster a diplomatic relationship with this likeable bane of the ninth, granted his request. Upon his return I ventured, 'Mr Stark, I hope that were you able to patronise our local latrines on this occasion?' To which comment came the reply, 'Yeah I was actually, and I seen them two spies you sent after me an' all.' He smiled – I simply roared. Time spent on reconnaissance is never wasted.

In keeping with the theme of toilet leave we must consider the case of Miss Jones and Miss Miller, who, frustrated at my repeated refusals to grant the former leave

– for it is known that children reckon a teacher's discipline by the ease with which they can remove themselves to the toilet – poured orange squash onto the wooden floor beneath Miss Jones's chair: 'I told you that she needed to go,' scolded Miss Miller, pointing to her friend, sobbing, head in arms, into her desk. I was profoundly grieved, and, until Miss Miller gave up the caper by laughing, most severely chastened. I considered the whole episode an excellent protest against the rules, worthy of much congratulation; naturally Miss Jones, having attained the laudable status of fool of the better sort, was excused on this occasion – but not before she had signed The Toilet Book, a subject upon which I will discourse more freely in a moment.

'Can I go to the toilet please?'
'Not in here you filthy beast: use the appointed facilities like everybody else. I dread to think what your bedroom is like.'

Interestingly enough, though, I have noted that around half of all applicants seeking to make water during lesson time can be dissuaded with the following question: 'If I do not let you go, will you wet yourself?' This is a question that surprisingly few scholars seem prepared to answer in the affirmative. The pupil who is prepared to announce confidently his probable incontinence is far more likely to be a genuine case for an entry in The Toilet Book. I offer this piece of advice only for cases in which the child in question is of the pubescent nemesis type; the teacher will of course use his discretion when petitioned by the meek or usually continent, or by those whom he knows to have good cause to be excused.

The Toilet Book is an excellent way of helping the selectively incontinent child to recognise that going to the toilet in lesson time is not an automatic right, and, once the serried ranks see this, fewer will chance a petition. Thus The Toilet Book, by reducing the number of frivolous requests, can be seen to champion the cause of the meek and needy, and is the very reverse of a tool of oppression.

The Toilet Book also has the effect of dissuading the likes of Mr Dorchester, who are simply trying to evade work and waste a few minutes in the corridor in that fellowship of miscreants. For the thought of actually having to write – in a book! – will ever prove contraceptive to his ablutions. Periodically tearing the full pages out of The Toilet Book enables the teacher to make quite ludicrous statements: 'You can count yourself very lucky, young man, you are only the sixth person I have allowed to visit the water closet during lesson time in over twenty-five years of teaching at this school.' It all helps.

It must also be noted that some of the most depraved and unmentionable acts performed on this earth are undertaken in school toilets during lesson time. Insisting on a record of who? and when? can only assist in guarding against such atrocities being performed with impunity.

I would like to take this opportunity to say that despite the slanders of my detractors, the Number One/Number Two column is entirely optional.

More sophisticated than an outright request to perform an ablution, however, is a request to obtain a tissue. The motive is the same: a few moments of freedom in the corridor and perhaps even chance congress with some like-minded idlers. What is different, though, is that while the teacher can discriminate against a child for not having used the toilets when they had the opportunity, it would be nothing short of barbaric to refuse someone the means to blow their nose, condemning them instead to yo-yo their dew drops in the company of others. The socially astute child is much aware of this loop-hole in educational law, so the teacher must ever be able politely to offer a box of tissues to those who would employ such sophistry to desert their seat of learning.

And so we can see from these toiletry examples that in order for privilege not to be degraded into a supposed right, which is the first stage of scholastic rebellion – and which all to often results in mundane foolishness – the vigilant teacher regards every action as one of at least potential insurrection. And while nice children should not be oppressed by a system that is designed to manage the rebelliousness of a minority, it must be acknowledged that this minority, though few in number, is large in influence, and capable of producing great and widespread misery for pupils and teachers alike. It is also important to note that this same minority, if badly managed, will soon become a large minority, and perhaps not even a minority. Even so, we do not wish to eradicate rebelliousness, for this a medium through which children develop independence and character; no, we mean only to raise the expression of rebelliousness to something nearer an artform, and to play our part in the development of a better kind of fool.

I have no small amount of sympathy for today's rebellious child; for rebelling is not as easy as it used to be. Permissiveness has taken away much of the old stamping ground – sex, drinking, drugs. What is a teenager supposed to rebel against these days? While adults are making their grotesque attempts at non-judgementalism, children are being driven to quite antisocial lengths just to get noticed, let alone create a sensation. Do not think the child grateful when we approve of his choice of clothes, and pretend to like his music; there is a chasm between generations that cannot be breached, and ought never to be even attempted. The child does not want the adult to approve of his rebellion – that rather defeats the object. The son does not want an invitation to smoke pot with his father, nor the daughter to scratch her name on the bus shelter bench alongside that of her mother. It is the job of the child to rebel, and it is the job of the adult to check and restrain this rebellion. Once this simple truth of education is understood, the job of teaching becomes far less mysterious.

> The man who teaches the young, who instils virtue into their minds (and we have a great shortage of good teachers), who grips and restrains those who are rushing madly after wealth and luxury, and if nothing more at least delays them – he too is doing a public service.

Seneca, 5BC–65AD

And is not rebellion – of the selfish and ignoble kind – little more than a rushing madly after wealth and luxury?

Children have got to rebel against something, and there is nothing in the life of a child – with the notable exception of his parents – that better lends itself to this purpose than school.

It never occurred to them to consider why such and such rules were laid down: the reason was nothing to them, and they only looked upon the rules as a sort of challenge from the rule makers, which it would be rather bad pluck of them not to accept.

Thomas Hughes, *Tom Brown's School Days*

Be sure that the child will always fastidiously keep his side of this arrangement; problems occur when teachers become too lazy, ignorant, busy or enlightened to keep theirs. Children sense quite brilliantly when no one is restraining them in their rebellious excesses, and the majority of behavioural problems in schools are caused by adults not acting in a way that children expect them to, and need them to. The rebellious youth longs to be rebuked; if he is not, he may rail against the loss of his rightful inheritance by becoming increasingly deviant. The incorrect shoe soon becomes the incorrect and dilatory shoe, which very soon becomes the shoe whose owner is not doing his homework and is becoming increasingly disruptive in class; and so it must continue until who knows what misery results? When the child has his act of rebellion acknowledged by an adult he gets his moment of infamy, and a happily low standard is set for future acts of rebellion. Recently, Mr Johnston remembered to me, from the wrong side of a fish-and-chip counter, that when he was a scholar under me, I had informed him that if he continued to wear grey laces in his shoes, he would probably end up in prison. The teacher knows his influence when his doctrines are remembered above his lessons, and, no doubt, Mr Johnston was, with tremendous love and tact, hinting at the fallibility of my predictions. But I, reaching for the late-night salt and vinegar, was already congratulating myself on my propheticism.

When rebellion first shows itself in visual signs, be sure that moral rebellion soon follows. Therefore, when Mr Green arrives bedecked in an assortment of cheap high-street fashions instead of his school uniform, he must be challenged. If he is not he is: a hero to the masses; a debaser of the innocent; an ornament of injustice; a menace to authority; and, to himself, one who must indulge in ever deepening insurrection to quench his lust for youthful rebellion. Ideally, Mr Green's state of dress would result in his instant removal from civil society before he could command adherents; however, I have noted that it is now often the case that the teacher is actually expected to countenance the vile discrepancy and teach the child nevertheless. In such cases, the miscreant should be made to suffer some small yet very public inconvenience, such as the loss of his usual seat, or a comment passed at his expense. This is of great moment, for if The Public Gaze discerns that no discomfort is visited upon the misdemeanant, the latter will, in a very short time indeed, command a following of the former.

Some years ago I discovered Mr Lansley chewing in class, and requested that he spit it out. On his way to the bin he swallowed the offending article and showed me his empty mouth with the considerable one-upmanship that is the very essence of childish rebellion. This mockery of his put me in a difficult position, and under The Public Gaze, too. However, I countered by having him stand over the bin, miming the spitting out of chewing gum. Very amusing, and I had him perform the act several times, that The Public Gaze might be more properly satisfied. Helping children to follow basic instructions is an important part of teaching, but so too is the acknowledgement of rebellion. By giving Mr Lansley his moment as the class coxcomb, while not swallowing, as it were, his slight upon my discipline, all parties – including that most demanding of audiences, The Public Gaze – were satisfied. I dread to think to what depraved and antisocial levels of rebelliousness the young scholar would have been driven had I not so brilliantly intervened.

I do not here have time to devote the proper amount of attention to the subject of chewing in class – for a book on that subject alone would be a weighty volume – but I will not deny the reader a few lines of advice on dealing with the menace. One vintage stratagem for the teacher to be vigilant of is The Division Of The Gum In The Mouth On The Way To The Bin strategem, in which only one half is ejected, leaving the exultant masticator to continue to ply his trade, albeit in reduced circumstances. A second deception is his leaning over the bin while giving it a light tap with his foot, creating the false impression of compliance through 'phantom emission'.

'Was it Copenhagen?'
'"There are two things that are infinite," said Einstein, "the universe and human stupidity." Volunteering an answer while masticating is exactly the kind of stupidity Einstein was talking about.'

Every school has its rebellious boys and girls to endure – adults have no say in that. However, adults do play a vital role in how that rebelliousness manifests itself. A climate where rebellion manifests itself in comparatively harmless breaches of the uniform code – a hat worn ominously to one side; a fat and low-slung tie; a carefully neglected button – punctuated occasionally by something quite spectacular or serious, is a far more educationally conducive climate than one of constant and tedious clichéd breaches of discipline; for the latter is the domain of the stupidly minded, where even the mundane fool can be king for a day.

When children perform even trifling transgressions the teacher should imply, by exhibiting the characteristics of one who is outraged and appalled, that they are transgressions of quite monstrous proportions. When the teacher exaggerates the severity of the wrongdoing the gullible child can be encouraged to conclude that he was far more deviant than he actually was. This is satisfactory to the teacher, the child, and The Public Gaze. The teacher ought to be fostering in children a healthy respect for wrongdoing, even while such wrongdoing continues to be done, and not, far more dangerously, a criminal flippancy. It is for this reason that we are particularly appalled at crimes committed 'in broad daylight', and prefer to see muggers running away from their victims, rather than sauntering.

'What! Not lined up? 'Tis worse than murder to do upon respect such violent outrage.'

Such exaggeration is, of course, pretence, but it does redeem the scholar from more serious rule-breaking: the public rebuke confirms the rebellion and the child is satisfied. The child need not move on to more serious acts, but will find future satisfaction at this level of rebellion. Thus, an unspoken code evolves whereby the teacher sets the level at which those children that need to demonstrate rebellion can do so, and the level remains constant. The teacher must be sure, though, always to acknowledge rebellion wherever and whenever he sees it, lest the stakes be raised against him.

> So the Romans saw when troubles were coming and always took counter measures. They never, to avoid a war, allowed them to go unchecked, because they knew that there is no avoiding war; it can only be postponed to the advantage of others.

Niccolò Machiavelli, *The Prince*

The teacher who waits for two boys to become bored of throwing pieces of rubber at each other waits in vain: he soon waits for three boys to become bored of throwing pieces of rubber at each other.

> In these instances, the Romans did what all wise rulers must: cope not only with present troubles but also with ones likely to arise in the future, and assiduously forestall them. When trouble is sensed well in advance it can easily be remedied; if you wait for it to show itself any medicine will be too late because the disease will have become

incurable. As doctors say of a wasting disease, to start with it is easy to cure but difficult to diagnose; after a time, unless it has been diagnosed and treated at the outset, it becomes easy to diagnose but difficult to cure.

Niccolò Machiavelli, *The Prince*

I am not advocating the teacher's following of every little incident to the same full and final conclusion; that would be exhausting, inhumane and counterproductive. What I am saying is that all acts of rebellion need to be acknowledged, and that there is acknowledgement – and therefore discipline – even in a raised eyebrow.

It is important for the teacher to understand that it is highly unusual for there to be status quo or equilibrium in child rebellion – things will either be getting more serious or less serious. This being understood, the teacher ought always to be reining in the wilful youth by ever reducing the number of ways in which he is 'allowed' – and I use this term poetically – to demonstrate his rebellion. The teacher need not fret over the child's liberty, or freedom of expression – children, when not stifled with too much freedom, are instinctively creative, and will encounter little difficulty in finding new schemes upon which to lavish their high-spiritedness. Therefore, the teacher who does no more than restrain the natural impulses of children improves the social and learning environment of his school and the sociability of its scholars, and plays his part in the production of a better kind of fool.

Of course uniform, upon which I will elaborate in the next chapter, is the best way to exert this salutary restraint upon the child because, in itself, it does not really matter. It is a practical, useful and harmless thing for the child to rebel against, so long as the teacher is seen to be outraged by its abuse. The school in which parading an untucked shirt represents an act of rebellion, and therefore draws the teacher's reproach, will typically see fewer fire-extinguishers set off than those with a more 'enlightened' position on uniform. Unfortunately, uniform is often regarded by teachers as a chore, rather than as the very useful tool that the sensible reader will, in the following chapter, see that it quite obviously is.

I do not suggest that every classroom can be made free of all difficult situations: into each life some rain must fall; the teacher is, after all, somebody who keeps the company of rapists, paedophiles, thieves and murderers some years before they are officially recognised as having fulfilled their potential. I wish only to show how the teacher, by understanding the positive role of rebellion in education, can avoid contributing to his own destruction. Often he will inherit problems of other people's making, and then there are always the unplayable deliveries that I will address in a moment; the teacher cannot reasonably be expected to be the solution to a problem that has been perhaps a decade or more in the making. This is why the Jesuit maxim reads, 'Give me a child until he is seven and

I will give you the man.' Remember to remind people who wish to lay blame at your door for the misbehaviour of their children, of the small proportion of their lives that you have influenced – or not. Much bad behaviour in the youth is the unhappy product of other people's laziness and stupidity, and yet the teacher is expected to manage, and dare I say instruct, the living manifestation of these miseries. The teacher will be warned, though, that those most culpable will not usually display gratitude when such things are pointed out to them.

> It may be reckoned amongst the vulgar errors, That too many suppose the whole care of their Children aught to be thrust upon the Master, and that Parents may totally neglect them; but it is high time for them to be sensible that there is a part to be done by them, which is no less necessary than reasonable; and 'twere to be wished that they would consider, That Masters undergo much more bootless and unprofitable toil, than would otherwise be requisite, if Parents would second the great attempt, and not grudge their auxiliary labours about those things which are within their sphere.

John Garretson, *The School of Manners*, 1701

I previously touched on the subject of unplayable deliveries, a term used by cricket commentators to describe a ball bowled so well that if the batsman tries to play it with the bat, he will certainly nick it and be caught behind; yet, if he leaves it to go harmlessly through to the wicket-keeper, it nicks the off stump. Some children are unplayable, usually through little fault of their own. There are children whom the teacher will not be able to defend his wicket against because, thankfully, they play by rules that he has never had to face: abuse, neglect, spoiling and parental separation head a sorry litany. The batsman that gets out to an unplayable delivery is never disgraced; in fact, he can expect a deal of sympathy on his walk off. The teacher must face his unplayable deliveries with decency; calmness of thought, word and deed; and in the knowledge that they do not come along often on good pitches. Then he should tuck his bat under his arm, nod approvingly, and trudge off to the pavilion. This he can do if he is secure in the knowledge that he has not just contributed to the loss of his own wicket. The batsman who recognises that his own ground staff are producing pitches that yield an uncommon number of unplayable deliveries may wish to change clubs.

One might conceive that it is bad form for the teacher to be bowled out so comprehensively while under The Public Gaze, but this is not so. Such an unhappy contingency is bound to occur occasionally when one considers that the teacher must ply his trade to hundreds of different personalities every week. In fact, if it was not for the goodwill, decency and obedience of so many of our young scholars, teaching would not be possible in the form we now do it. The teacher can only use the protocols in place, and, no matter how unsatisfactory they may be, he must let the system – which has (or ought to have) more weight than he does – do its work. He should not suffer in silence, but should have his senior colleagues – who have won promotion and financial reward upon the bold claims of what they claim to know, and intend to do – make good on these claims. If this does not happen in a reasonable period of time, the teacher would be well advised either to resign his post and find a new school, or lower his standards and reconcile himself to circumstances.

Unplayable deliveries – if the teacher be not an instrument of his own destruction – are clearly beyond the control of the teacher, and even The Public Gaze does not expect any more than that he keep his dignity and demonstrate pity over anger. Children are perceptive, and can differentiate between the deviancy of social neglect and that of tyranny. Whereas the latter might command a following, the former more often commands pity: there is a difference between an untucked shirt and an unwashed shirt. When Mr White comes to my lesson wearing trainers again, and without an excuse slip, again, I give him the choice of either going to his tutor or leaving his offending shoes at the door. Being the kind of boy who wears the wrong uniform out of a sense of hopelessness, rather than insurrection, he opts to work in his socks.

Children are a blessing, says Solomon in Psalm 127, something completely endorsed in Proverbs, with one important qualification: if they are to be a blessing they must be wise children. Solomon was an educational realist, in that he knew that a teacher's best efforts can be ignored: he can only advise, and not enforce. The scholar, if lacking in wisdom, can reject his teacher's efforts to improve him, and the very best teachers and parents of every generation have suffered at the hands of unhealthily rebellious children. We may well pose the question, why do good teachers have bad pupils? And yet even if we were to arrive at answers to that question we will soon discover that those answers offer us no practicable solutions to the problems. We might, however, take comfort in remembering that Jesus had for one of his pupils a certain Judas Iscariot, and they do not come much worse than that. We all, it seems, have our crosses to bear – or not.

Uniform

You're gonna get it for looking different.

Johnny Rotten (on being beaten up by skinheads as a young punk)

I am reminded of the outrage of a lady colleague who was used, quite brazenly, by a wayward scholar with a bold approach to the problem (as he saw it) of school uniform. This scholar had asked the teacher in question, at the end of the school day, if he might be afforded the privacy of her stock cupboard to change out of his school clothes, which, she noted, were a rather rough translation of those stipulated by the school. Having given her permission, and expectant of seeing him emerge in the very latest cheap high-street fashions, she was outraged to see the scoundrel reappear in perfect school uniform – black shoes and all! – and ready to reacquaint himself with his parents. These parents were seconding at home that which was not even being attempted in the first place at

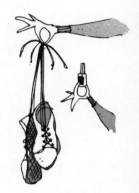

'Could you put a bit of whitening on these by tomorrow morning, please?'

school. Walter Bagehot wrote, 'A school master should have an atmosphere of awe, and walk wonderingly, as if he was amazed at being himself.' Yet surely these qualities belong to the fourteen-year-old scholar who manages, at a single stroke, to ridicule both his parents and his teachers, and get help into the bargain.

Readers of the previous chapter will already appreciate the vital role played by uniform as a foil to rebellion.

> The boys were scruffier, coarser, dirtier, everything about them indicated a planned conformity – the T-shirts, jeans, haircuts, the same wary sullenness. None of it really belonged to them. It was worn, assumed in and out of school like a kind of armour; a gesture against authority; a symbol of toughness as thin and synthetic as the cheap films from which it was copied.

E.R. Braithwaite, *To Sir, With Love*

If uniform were to serve no other purpose than to provide the child with something to rebel against, it would be worth pursuing for this cause alone – and much misery prevented. I am aware, however, of eight further purposes served by school uniform, and these purposes, some moral and some practical, form the basis of this chapter. Here I assert that school uniform is not a needless and antiquated tradition, but the logical answer to many difficult questions, arrived at by clear educational thinking.

But first, another perceptive observation from Mr Braithwaite.

> They nearly all wore a kind of unofficial uniform. Among the girls, proud of bust and uplift brassiere, this took the form of too-tight sweaters and too-long clingy skirts and flat heeled shoes. A wide variety of hairstyles paid tribute to their particular screen favourite. It was all a bit soiled and untidy, as if too little attention were paid to washing either themselves or their flashy finery. The boys wore blue jeans and T-shirts or open-necked plaid shirts.

E.R. Braithwaite, *To Sir, With Love*

The majority of children, then, *want* to wear a uniform to school – one of their own design, it must be admitted, but a uniform nonetheless. If they are not made to wear somebody else's, they will happily wear one of their own conception.

Ask the teacher why his school has a uniform code and he will probably say that it has something to do with prevention of bullying. This, sadly, is indicative of the lack of thought that is devoted to the subject of school uniform, and would explain the current dearth of understanding of it within the teaching profession. Why is it that for hundreds of years schools have persisted in their attempts, to a greater and lesser extent and effect, to compel the children under their charge to wear a set of clothes that invariably, and quite evidently, they do not want to wear? Is it, as those of a more enlightened disposition would have us believe, simply a form of scholastic repression, invented by our forefathers as an accompaniment to the thick ear and the cane? Or is there something slightly more productive and purposeful in it, something that might be worth remembering, or rediscovering?

Some teachers fail to realise that uniform is for their benefit *and* that of their pupils. When such teachers are asked for their views on school uniform they might say, 'Why does it matter? What difference does it make to a child's education whether they are wearing black trainers or black shoes?' Uniform, the great friend of the teacher, has, for many, become an unnecessary and misunderstood chore. Be sure, though, that the wayward scholar has not become any less clear of his obligations to the school uniform. One could hardly expect him to uphold the idea and standard of a school uniform, and it would be a pretty poor school where he did. The approach of the child towards the challenge of evading school uniform (and don't children invariably rise to such challenges) has, therefore, become ever more sophisticated, in inverse proportion to his teachers' ever-dwindling resolve.

And so, over the years, we have witnessed V-necks become sweatshirts, black shoes become black trainers, black trainers white trainers; whilst fly-browing, tramlining, piercing and general accessorising have increased to epidemic proportions. I have, with my own eyes, seen scholars reluctant to lift the pens in their hands for the weight of paraphernalia attached to their wrists.

In order to evaluate the proper role and effectiveness of school uniform, we must begin by answering the questions raised a few moments ago. Why does school uniform matter? What difference does it make to a child's education? What is it that makes a black shoe educationally superior to a white one? Since the only significant difference between a black trouser and a black jean, for instance, is in the pocket, and since one pocket cannot be proven to be educationally superior to another, how can it possibly matter what trouser a child wears? Clearly these external furnishings have no direct influence on the brain or mind, so why bother with school uniform at all? Why not do away with it and focus on things that might really make a difference to the education of a child?

But let us consider the pocket that distinguishes the jean from the trouser. It is obvious yet necessary to understand that it is not the stylistic peculiarities of the pocket that are important, but what that pocket style represents; one style representeth that which is righteous, and good, and the other that which is unrighteous, and leads to waywardness. The fact that the decision over what is deemed right or wrong is completely subjective is as unimportant as who makes the decision. All that matters is that somebody in absolute authority has made a decision that, in a particular school, some clothes are right and some clothes are wrong. So long as the maker of such a decision refuses to be moved, this value judgement becomes an absolute judgement, and a non-negotiable uniform is established. This kind of absolutism is rare in our post-modern society, yet while one scholar delights in it because it gives him something definite to rebel against, another delights in it because it shows him exactly what not to do to keep out of trouble.

Furthermore, because being asked to wear a uniform is not an unreasonable request – like it or not, many employers do require a uniform – only a person who does not necessarily believe that he should work for a living would say that it is. Uniform is a reality in the same way that queuing is. Show me a person who thinks that school uniform is unreasonable and I will very probably be able to show you a person who does not necessarily believe that when he joins a queue, he should join it at the back.

But does uniform have any practical uses besides giving children something to rebel against? I mentioned that there are eight other reasons for advocating school uniform. I will now address each of these.

1 Everybody wants to be free, especially the youth, for he has not yet realised that society is not free. We are all tied into a system of bondage for the supposed common good, whether you believe in it or not. Any educational establishment concerned in the preparation of young persons for adult life must see the importance of exposing those same children to one of life's grim truths; namely, that often in life one must either be doing that which one has been told to do, or not doing that which one has been told not to do.

> The whole timetable in this school is meant to help you in the world after you leave here, and doing what you are told in spite of not liking it, is part of that training.

E.R. Braithwaite, *To Sir, With Love*

Now a person may consider himself free to ignore the law; if caught, however, he will quickly discover that the consequences are not similarly optional; so it should be with school uniform. Any scholastic establishment that does not preach the doctrine that to have more freedom than sense is an unfortunate thing is a wicked scholastic establishment.

IF I Entered a restricted area in
an airport I WOULD GO to
PRISON

IF I entered a restricted area in
an airport I would go to
PRISON

Uniform sets the tone for an improvement process that may, at times, require unquestioning obedience. Often the child does not know what is good for him and may vigorously rail against such a call for conformity. When he deliberately refuses to wear the school uniform he is demonstrating, firstly, a belief that the school institution is working directly against his personal interest, and secondly, an intention to thwart the school's efforts. It is an act of open defiance against a system that has his long-term well-being, if not his short-term desires, at heart. There is a time and a place for revolt and disobedience, but it needs to be reserved for more important issues than simply getting one's own way. Few of us, for instance, in the day-to-day world of the workplace would make much headway with an attitude of blind disobedience: the construction worker who decides not to wear his hat may look forward to an extended opportunity to tend his garden. Uniform is a tool for getting the child prepared for an improvement process wherein he is not an expert, and where he would benefit from occasional compliance with the statutes of those who are.

2 School uniform demonstrates to the child the need to keep his focus on improving his character, and not his aesthetic; the adult should ever be urging the child to lessen his commitment to non-mattering things. The teacher must guard against the child worrying unduly about what he is going to wear to school, guiding him instead to nurture improvements that will benefit those with whom he must work and play. Albert Einstein is said to have purchased many versions of the same suit, shirt and shoes when he went clothes shopping. This he did so that instead of expending brain power on choosing what to wear each morning, he could put his mind to more noble pursuits. He often went un-socked, believing, one presumes, the sock to be of insignificant intellectual value. For a similar reason did William Cobbett offer the following invective against mirrors, in his splendidly titled book *Advice to Young Men, and (Incidentally) to Young Women, in the Middle and Higher Ranks of Life*:

> A looking-glass is a piece of furniture a great deal worse than useless. Looking at the face will not alter its shape or its colour; and, perhaps, of all wasted time, none is so foolishly wasted, as that which is employed in surveying of one's own face.

It is quite natural for the scholar, wayward or otherwise, to worry about what he will wear to school, and how he will be perceived by his peers, but he is worrying for reasons which the adult should, at the very least, be disdainful of. Mr Cobbett, again:

> This sort of extravagance, this waste of money on the decoration of the body, arises solely from vanity, and from vanity of the most contemptible sort. It arises from the notion, for instance, that all the people in the street will be looking at you as soon as you walk out; and that they will, in a greater or less degree, think better of you on account of your fine dress. Never was notion more false. All the sensible people that happen to see you will think nothing at all about you: those that are filled with the same vain notion as you are will perceive your attempt to impose on them, and will despise you accordingly: rich people will wholly disregard you, and you will be envied and hated by those who have the same vanity that you have without the means of gratifying it.

Whether it be dandyism, glorious defiance, or fear of being ostracised by his own, once a child becomes accepted by his peers ostensibly for his physical appearance he rather typically, and somewhat understandably, sees less the need to develop the integrity and nobility of his mind. Furthermore, I maintain it to be an observable fact that peer pressure hinders many scholars from doing as well at their classes as they otherwise might – or at least from being seen to. Since peer groups are underpinned by collective fashion statements, incorrect school uniform necessarily becomes first an advert for, and then a cause of, underachievement. Of course it is not reasonable for adults to expect children to realise this, or even to care about it: the wayward scholar would much prefer to be popularly acclaimed amongst his own than academically acclaimed by his teachers – and thank goodness for that! No, the corrosive consequences of aesthetic underachievement need to be combated through the rigorous enforcement of a school uniform, because for each and every scholar who is indulged in only an interpretation of what has been stipulated, there will be many others in the mobile majority silently making plans to be similarly indulged. And while each one is contemplating the excuses that he is going to tell his parents and his tutor, he is not focusing on self-improvement of the more noble and selfless kind. A boy oppressed with what he will wear to school carries in his head a mind that is quite useless for intellectual labours.

An insistence on school uniform is the teacher's enactment of a belief that no sensible person would oppose: namely, that the person matters more than his clothes. We should not expect this enactment to lessen the wayward scholar's dedication to high-street trifles, but we should want to give very clear notice of how trivial such values are held by sensible people. The teacher who does not very clearly demonstrate his disdain for sartorial ostentation through an insistence on school uniform cannot count himself to be on the side of the oppressed. Uniform is necessary to remind some people that they are not as important as they think they are, and to cause us all to be ever mindful that the individual is sometimes significantly less, and sometimes significantly more, than his clothes would suggest. Albert Einstein said, when his wife asked him to change clothes to meet the German Ambassador, 'They want to see me, here I am. If they want to see my clothes, open my closet and show them my suits.'

Every scholar has his priorities, and these must necessarily seem very important to him; but where physical appearance is high on that list, the adult must attempt to challenge this attitude in the scholastic setting through the rigid enforcement of a school uniform. The child that grows up to rate his own aesthetic highly will also, let us not forget, disdain the appearance of others, poisoning not just his own growth but the growth of those who come into contact with him.

> If most of us are ashamed of shabby clothes and shoddy furniture, let us be more ashamed of shabby ideas and shoddy philosophies…It would be a sad situation if the wrapper were better that the meat wrapped inside it.
>
> **Albert Einstein**

3 While Mr Einstein is quite right to remind us that a showy wrapper will not improve the taste of the meat enclosed – will not make us better people – we must

remember that there are norms of dress. People will often form their immediate opinions of us based on how we differ, or correspond to, the social norm for any given setting. These norms are neither good nor bad, they are merely a fact of life. There are norms of dress for pubs, for clubs and for places of work, and it is the teacher's duty to prepare children better for the latter than the former. Making judgements based on appearance is flawed, and open to abuse and misinterpretation, but it does at least suggest the possibility that a particular norm is held by the wearer; and, if it is a value that is but lightly held, is of at least potential use to him who must weigh a stranger. The fact that we are all shallow enough to judge and be judged by appearances is a disconcerting truth, and yet it is a truth, and must be owned as such. This is, after all, why we dress smartly for a job interview, and why it is unlikely that some hitchhikers will ever find a lift. Even the defendant that approaches the judge dressed in a suit has learned something of the ways of the world.

The youth who acknowledges all of this and yet replies, 'I will be judged by my own,' will need to be reminded that, in the first instance at least, 'his own' will not give him a job; and is it not the wish of every teacher to see those in his charge make their way by their own labours, and not by the sweat of another's brow? I am reminded of two applicants for teaching posts, one who failed to be selected after – perhaps purely incidentally – wearing black training shoes to his interview, and another, who also did not get selected, but this time quite specifically on account of his not filling his belt loops with the belt that they were so clearly meant to encompass. Mock if you will, this is the way of the world and it is better to know it and scorn it than simply to scorn it. Furthermore, I believe that those who offer jobs have every right to insist that their own standards of dress are met, however obscure they may appear to the rest of us. After all, why should the employer take what he would consider to be unnecessary risks? Uniform gets a person prepared for work: and is it not useful employment that gives a person independence, keeps him from being a burden to others, allows him choices, and gives him the means to raise a family – something without which no honest person should procreate; is not useful employment, I say, a very important goal of every sensible educationalist?

4 I have noted that some of our young ladies have used a laxness in uniform to occasion their undergarments to be seen in public: a suggestion, one presumes, of a particularly liberated moral outlook with which, for some reason, they wish to be associated. One does not have to go looking for such things: the teacher might easily make such an unhappy discovery when, for instance, pencils etc. are retrieved from the floor, or when stretching occurs to relieve boredom.

I did on one occasion, when the G-string had been played particularly bombastically in my direction by a youth belonging to that socio-intellectual group from which glamour models emerge, counter with Proverbs 11:22: 'As a jewel of gold in a swine's snout, so is a fair woman which is without discretion.' The aforementioned sermon I delivered with the utmost circumspection: for it is a dangerous state of affairs for the teacher to reveal to the schoolgirl that he has just witnessed her thong. Furthermore, many has been the time – and quite without my having wished it, I can assure you – that I have seen printed about the waistband of the undergarment the word Monday, or Tuesday, even though it had been a Thursday or a Friday, and though this was certain to be nothing more than a laundering anomaly, or an infelicity of selection, the mind misgives!

The less the teacher's commitment to the cause of school uniform, the greater the breaches of impropriety and respectability. Instances such as the two that I have just quite delicately described would be far less possible, and therefore much less probable, if a robust school uniform were in place.

5 A hugely important but oft overlooked facet of school uniform is that it aids creative development through rebellion, and although much of what I might have said here has been said in the first chapter, I will add a few more words. If a child is to be creative and purposeful

in his rebellion, adults have a role in stimulating this creativity through a limitation of his options. If I ask you to write a poem for me about whatever you wish, you will probably have difficulty in knowing what to write. But if I include all manner of restrictions, such as it having to be a haiku about a three-legged pig that has escaped from the squire's sty, you would be far more likely to arrive at something like this:

> Halt porcine tripod;
> Attend your swinish house now!
> Consider Gent's roast.

Children ought to be encouraged in the belief that rebelling against the school uniform is a big deal. The best way to achieve this is by teachers making a hue and cry when it is breached. The aim is to keep the wayward scholar bumbling along in the foothills of mischief, not scaling Everest; a happy by-product of this arrangement is that it can raise the standard of youth rebellion, and stimulate creativity. It has been suggested by some learned commentators that the decay of social and moral constraints, in spite of allowing us great personal freedom and choice, has meant that we may well have seen the end of true creative genius in our time. Anybody wishing to test the veracity of such a conjecture may wish to consider the fruits of modern art, or the giftedness of some of our most venerated celebrities: too little freedom, it would appear, is a more likely aid to creative genius than too much. Certainly the teacher will want the scholar to express himself as an individual while at school, but as an individual far more creative than is allowed for by the hackneyed white training shoe, the ubiquitous hooped earring, or the jean-pocketed trouser.

6 Uniform keeps power where it is least likely to be abused, and restrains, if nothing more, the conditions under which bullying thrives. Power in the classroom is an uncomfortable concept about which to write, and yet the role of uniform in the shaping of the power struggle needs to be made clear. Since compliance with school uniform is an admission of subordination, the scholar who wants to demonstrate to his teachers and friends that he has aspirations to accrue power for himself often does so first by refusing to wear the uniform. If he is allowed to remain in this state of corrupted undress then this aspiration has been actuated, and he has grown in power. This of course is quite obvious, but less obvious is where his newly gained power comes from. Does it come from a previously untapped reserve? No, it does not, because power in a school is a finite resource; it can change hands, but, as with energy in the first law of thermodynamics, it cannot be created or destroyed: one cannot lock power in the stock cupboard, and even if one could, the person holding the key would control it. So, to return to the question of where the wayward scholar gets his power: he gets it from

his teacher. As the miscreant becomes ever more powerful through being seen, through his lack of school uniform, to be above the law, so the teacher becomes conspicuously impotent, as his authority is seen to drain from him and pass to another. And if the teacher does not at first notice his loss, he soon will; for power is a very attractive quality and quickly commands a following. Therefore, wherever uniform is stipulated but not maintained, the teacher in that school will suffer both a loss of authority and an increase in the difficulty of his daily work.

Power in the right hands is a good thing because it brings peace. Classrooms where the power lies in the hands of a responsible and, let us hope, reasonable adult, rather than in the hands of the wayward scholar and his adherents, are, I suggest, the more pleasant and educationally conducive classrooms. Power in the hands of young people is almost never pleasant – it quickly finds its way into the wrong sort of young hands and typically results in unkindness. Some of the most unkind things said and done on this earth are said and done by schoolchildren, who, in the words of Mr Chips, are 'decent little beggars individually, but as a mob, just pitiless and implacable.'

> Roger led the way straight through the castles, kicking them over, burying the flowers, scattering the chosen stones.
> Maurice followed, laughing, and added to the destruction.

William Golding, *Lord of the Flies*

Lord of the Flies is only notionally fictitious.

For what reason other than brutal unkindness was Mr Garrick witnessed to have liberally bespeckled his face with large dots from a marker pen before laying it down in front of his hardworking neighbour, Mr Warburton, and exclaiming, 'Sir, look what Aaron did to me!' It was within the power of young Mr Garrick to bring misery into the life of Mr Warburton, and he therefore attempted the doing of it. It is by no means, however, only children that suffer under the cruelty of misappropriated power.

Dear sir
I'm very sorry for calling you an Hampster I didn't mean it and it will not happen again
yours sincearly

My behaivior is unspeckable I do not no how you put up with it but you do so, that means you are doing a good job. I will try to behaive in class alot more and I will work alot harder.

The scholar must come to the conclusion that belonging to the uniform wearing cohort is in his best interest. The penalties for being a renegade must far outweigh the delight and associated kudos attendant on the rebel; good must always be seen to triumph, and those that conform should ever feel the inner warmth of having made the right choice. Schools that allow some children to defile the morality of the uniform code encourage wickedness and oppression: for uniform codes that are allowed to degenerate end up simply denoting the compliantly weak from the mutinously strong. Bullying flourishes in such a climate. Indeed it would be far better to have no uniform code at all than for a weak and lazy attempt at it to be seen, so publicly, to fail. Bullying ever has and ever will be a problem in all scholastic establishments; yet the school that does not uphold its uniform code – if it has one – contributes significantly to that problem. It is mindless folly to lament the presence of bullying in schools when the conditions under which it thrives have not, as far as is institutionally possible, been eradicated. People who say that the case for uniform centres on the need for wealth – or, more specifically, the lack of it – to be made inconspicuous see only the tip of the iceberg. The real function of uniform, as far as it relates to bullying, is one that centres on power.

7 I wish to point out that while poor uniform is often a symptom of a bad attitude, it very quickly becomes a major cause of it. It creates in the child a lethargy to all rules and standards of behaviour, and produces a downward spiral of harmfulness.

8 I made mention earlier of my belief that uniform is a great friend to the teacher; this is because uniform is a medium through which troublemakers generously identify themselves. It is of enormous benefit to schools to have their most difficult scholars give, through their choice of clothes, such unequivocal notice of their intention to tread the path of waywardness. The ability to spot troublemakers with ease is a great asset to both the individual teacher and the headteacher, because it allows for proactive measures to be taken, instead of only reactive ones: follow the boy wearing jean-pocketed trousers and be there on the scene when he does it! Furthermore, uniform abuse helps in the fight against crime, because the teacher knows from where instances of villainy are most likely to issue, both within the classroom and around the school. When riot police seek to break up a disturbance and are vastly outnumbered, they scan the crowd for the rabble-rousers and arrest them first. Once these powerful individuals have been removed from the scene, the flock of followers lose their rallying-points and begin to drift away. The scholastic miscreant does the teacher a great courtesy when he so readily identifies himself, and the teacher does everyone concerned a terrible disservice when he pretends not to notice.

I noted in Chapter 1 that a status quo does not exist in schools: all things are either improving or slipping. Since I have never noted improvement to arise out of negligence – perhaps with the notable exception of the discovery of penicillin – the battle to uphold school uniform needs must be a continuous one. It is not a war that any teacher or school can ever claim a final victory in, but an eternal one, the battles of which must be fought dozens of times a day, and on many fronts simultaneously. Absolute victory is never achieved but the teacher is forever shifting the barricades forward, in anticipation of the day when the battle will rage over top buttons.

Few things in school sadden me more than the words 'uniform crackdown'. A uniform crackdown inevitably means picking on the nice children who have got the right shoes at home, and who will be wearing them tomorrow if told, instead of tackling the chronic offenders whose complete disregard for the school rules means that they do not even own the right shoes, because they lied to their mothers in the shoe shop. A uniform crackdown also tends to result in perfection being demanded from those likely to produce it, while a slightly more fanciful excuse than usual is apparently the accepted gesture from a more difficult case with a hard dad. No doubt the more perspicacious of my readers will already have noticed the worthy role that a uniform crackdown plays in the very generous provision of easy-to-spot victims for our school bullies. Even more serious, though, is that a uniform crackdown is a public confirmation of an institution's irreverence for its own rules. I consider it most unreasonable that the young scholar is expected to reverence rules that must necessarily be held in very low regard by their legislators; for if they were not held in low regard a uniform crackdown would not be required. The uniform crackdown is synonymous with previous weakness and failure, and serves only to advertise this ineffectiveness. Fuelled on emotion, and creating utterly avoidable hostility, a uniform crackdown has none of the effectiveness of low-key, day-to-day intolerance of uniform abuse and rule-breaking in general. I have sympathy with the malcontented teacher who might object to school uniform on the basis of the harmful confrontation that it provokes between teacher and scholar; however, this confrontation is not the fault of school uniform per se, but rather an unhappy symptom of its poor implementation.

The zero-tolerance approach and its effectiveness in improving behaviour are exemplified by the Broken Windows Theory. This states that if one broken window in a building is left unrepaired, soon all the windows will be broken. I have seen such buildings with my own eyes and, though it was long ago, may even have contributed to the development of one.

Well I very much subscribe to the Broken Windows Theory
that was developed by Professors Wilson and Kelling,
25 years ago maybe. The idea of it is that you had to pay
attention to small things, otherwise they would get out of
control and become much worse…So we started paying
attention to the things that were being ignored. Aggressive
panhandling, the squeegee operators that would come
up to your car and wash the window of your car whether
you wanted it or not – and sometimes smashed people's
cars or tires or windows – the street-level drug dealing;
the prostitution; the graffiti, all these things that were
deteriorating the city. So we said, 'We're going to pay
attention to that.'

Rudolph Giuliani, Mayor of New York

And pay attention to that he did. Turnstile jumpers on the
subway were arrested and chained together for avoiding the
$1.25 fare; trains that returned to the depot with new graffiti
on them were not allowed back out until they had been
cleaned; squeegee kids were driven from the streets; and
as a consequence serious crime plummeted too. It did not
plummet because the serious criminals looked at what was
happening and were afraid of getting caught; it plummeted
because they already had been caught: the serious criminals
were also the petty criminals. That is why it is imperative
that the teacher pays attention to everything.

A want of adherence to a school's uniform code is
a springboard into a cesspool of antisocial behaviour,

including such miseries as tardiness, penlessness and book-lessness; for I have well noted that the wayward scholar does not usually delight in the management of these areas while making free with his school's uniform policy. Having achieved an understanding of the flexibility of the uniform rule he will, quite correctly, go on to apply this interpretation to many other rules.

With regard to penal intervention, one might, in respect of his sartorial disobedience, levy against him an after-school detention every day of the week; but ultimately, if he is allowed to be at large during the day, with all of the associated glory and might, he will, quite rightly, consider himself to be getting the best of the bargain: for what is an inconvenience served behind a closed door, and after hours, when compared to a public display of power to his own people, and in the broadest of daylight too?

Schools invent impractically sophisticated schemes to crack age-old problems, but they are simply neither efficient nor effective. It is worth remembering that big problems rarely start off as big problems. The school that attends upon lateness, chewing-gum under tables, queue jumping, littering, graffiti and uniform will not find that the more serious issues disappear; they will, however, find them drastically reduced in number, and far easier to spot. There are, though, as Eisenhower said, no victories at discount prices, and all things must be attended to at all times.

A wise prince must observe these rules; he must never take things easy in times of peace, but rather use the latter assiduously, in order to be able to reap the profit in times of adversity. Then, when his fortunes change, he will be found ready to resist adversity.

Niccolò Machiavelli, *The Prince*

But the uniform issue goes deeper than simply catching and disciplining, it is also concerns justice, and the need to give those who are compliant a sense of having made a sensible choice. This is the battle for the mobile majority – that lump of scholars that simply want safety, and know that safety can only be secured by siding with the most powerful faction in the classroom. The school where the wayward scholar is given a sense of immunity, and is therefore allowed to accrete power, offers no such safety, and must be prepared to inherit classrooms of strife.

Fear

He who fears dangers does not perish by them.

Leonardo da Vinci

In the previous chapter, we have seen the need for the teacher to recruit the mobile majority – that unresolved mass of political turncoats looking to align themselves with the most powerful group or individual in the classroom. Let us consider, then, how the teacher might shape circumstances to ensure that he is that power. There are, broadly speaking, two ways in which the teacher employs himself in this battle for the undecided: firstly, by what he does, a subject that will be more thoroughly developed in the chapter on discipline; and secondly, by that which he tacitly threatens to do. The latter may also be referred to under the umbrella term of 'fear', and an understanding of this oft-misunderstood concept must inform our discussion. The reader will also find a significant portion of this chapter devoted to a thing called 'shouting', for without slipper or cane this has often been used – sometimes with good effect, sometimes bad – as a substitute for those former methods of correction.

Perhaps the most practical piece of advice on the subject of fear is found in Machiavelli's *The Prince*, the Renaissance guide on how a prince should take and hold a small kingdom. I have never quite come to understand why Sig. Machiavelli's name has become so inextricably associated with perfidy. It seems to me that rather than laud him for his insight into some uncomfortable truths of human nature, posterity has decided to despise him for bringing them to our attention. Certainly classrooms do work in the same way as did those Italian city-states about which he wrote.

> From this arises the following question: whether it is better to be loved than feared, or the reverse. The answer is that one would like to be both the one and the other; but because it is difficult to combine them, it is far better to be feared than loved if you cannot be both…Men worry less about doing an injury to one who makes himself loved than to one who makes himself feared…The prince must…make himself feared in such a way that, if he is not loved, at least he escapes being hated. For fear is quite compatible with an absence of hatred.
>
> **Niccolò Machiavelli,** *The Prince*

Does not every fond recollection of a favourite teacher follow the wisdom of the last sentence? Does one ever hear, 'He was soft, and we mocked him openly, and messed around endlessly – I loved that man'? Let this, then, advise the teacher who would wish to be liked: be feared first, and liked – hopefully – later.

There needs must be an element of fear in the classroom because, like the city-states on which Machiavelli advised, the classroom operates through fear. Fear is essentially the diplomatic arm of power, and a fear of things dreaded protects us from the power that may bring such things to pass. For the purposes of so small a kingdom as a classroom, we can, without injury to any but mere definers of terms, use the words power and fear interchangeably. When well managed, power brings peace and safety to the classroom; but if allowed to fall into the hands of a wayward scholar, it leads first to anarchy and then to oppression.

> When the righteous are in authority, the people rejoice: but when the wicked beareth rule, the people mourn.
>
> **Proverbs 29:2**

The wayward scholar senses unerringly when there is little to be feared, and he and his adherents are experts in appropriating, for their own misuse, the power of a careless teacher. The teacher who would seek to practise without encouraging in the scholars a little fear of himself should consider that he does not banish power from his classroom, he merely places his own stock into the hands of another, who, in exercising his guardianship of it, may bring about much misery. Is it not far better for a responsible adult to administer appropriate discipline to those who deserve it than for the class to disintegrate into an oaf's paradise, where bodily or verbal meanness – so often the product of newly gained power – is meted out by scoundrels on a might-is-right basis? Let us not fall into the habit of immediately associating fear and power with violence and bullying; for what the wayward scholar (not the irretrievably lost one) dreads above all is parental contact. The teacher who has a reputation for doing such things is much feared when he threatens this, and if he always delivers on his threats wields tremendous power to lessen waywardness. Somebody is going to be the most powerful and most feared individual in the classroom, of that the teacher has no choice; but if not the teacher, then who? Fear creates order, and order creates safety. The classroom where the teacher is an object of open ridicule is not a safe place for the steady scholar to be; for it is only a matter of time before he too becomes an object of somebody's ridicule or abuse. A teacher must seem dangerous, for if he does not, he will almost certainly seem ridiculous; and is there anything that quite so readily lends itself to humour as a person in a position of authority who clearly has no authority? Please consider the national predilection for the appropriation of policemen's helmets, and the case of the unfortunately named Mr Rule:

I must not out run mr Rule
I must not out run mr Rule
I must not out run mr Rule
I must not out run mr Rule

However, an appetite for power is certainly not a healthy desire for the teacher to harbour, and we would be deeply suspicious of one who confessed as his motivation for becoming a teacher the fantastic opportunities for ordering children about. No matter how well intentioned, an appetite for power tends to lead to suffering for somebody. The teacher ought to accept the burden of power reluctantly, aiming to have the maximum amount of authority with the minimum amount of power; this is how it should be with the judge. The judge has very little power of his own; he cannot indulge his own extravagances, he can only apply the laws that he has been given. And yet because those laws carry with them – or ought to – the weight of the people, he has tremendous authority when he applies them. A judge is not seen to shout or get angry, because these qualities are not necessary for the application of the law. He may of course become angry in his private chamber, or even in the courtroom, but here the anger is simply a by-product of his personal displeasure, and is not required for the administration of justice.

Nor had I ever met before perfect courtesy in a teacher. It had nothing to do with softness; Smewgy could be very severe, but it was the severity of a judge, weighty and measured, without taunting…

C.S. Lewis, *Surprised By Joy*

If the teacher can comport himself in the manner of a judge, then he can hold his power and authority in such a way as it ought to be held. But in order for this to be possible, the entire system of educational law and justice needs to be thorough, fair and rigorously upheld; instead, however, we find that they are often not. When the teacher lacks faith in the authority of his superiors, he is far more likely to be forced into circumstances where he feels compelled to rely on his own power: misery, in one of its many unforeseen manifestations, is invariably the outcome for both scholar and teacher. A lack of hierarchical rigour or competence, though, is not an acceptable reason (though it is, perhaps, an excuse) for the teacher to increase his anger at the wayward scholar, who is, after all, only trying to get away with whatever he can. This is what children do, and adults ought well to know it. No, the teacher's anger would be more properly directed at poor administrators and sloppy administrations, and the injustices that they produce, than at the natural tendencies of children.

But I must remember the subject upon which I have chosen to discourse, and not trespass too far from the issue of fear by leaving you to consider the disciplinary practice of Mr Alworthy, that father to the foundling Tom Jones:

> It was Mr Alworthy's custom never to punish any one,
> not even to turn away a servant, in a passion. He resolved
> therefore to delay passing sentence on Jones till the
> afternoon.

Henry Fielding, *Tom Jones*

Classrooms cannot function properly when based upon the whims and wills of so many scholars, their behaviour changing even with the wind and the moon. The classroom requires a powerful yet responsible leader to create calm, safe and purposeful conditions. Despite what some of our more enlightened experts may hold to be the innate virtue of youth, massed children are rarely capable of achieving this by themselves; it is an unfortunate truth that wayward scholars in teacherless classrooms behave very much like so many animals in a pack:

> For boys follow one another in herds like sheep, for good
> or evil; they hate thinking, and have rarely any settled
> principles.

Thomas Hughes, *Tom Brown's School Days*

This is of great moment to the teacher, and I urge his most particular attention. In every class there is a great lump of undecided souls who are as yet unsettled upon how they are going to behave, and who are looking to ally themselves to a leader. They will not give their support away for nothing, however; the payment that they desire is security. It follows, therefore, that this mobile majority will usually side with the most dangerous individual or dominant group in the classroom, for this is the safest thing to do in order to avoid oppression. Therefore, it can be seen that the most dangerous person in the room – and we might as well say the most feared – commands the mobile majority. Children want safety from oppression, but, more importantly, they want safety from oppression by their own – that is, other children.

> Hardly any amount of oppression from above takes the heart out of a boy like oppression from his fellows.

C.S. Lewis, *Surprised By Joy*

This means that the teacher is at a significant disadvantage when he attempts to win for himself the mobile majority, for his favour is not so keenly sought as that of the scholastic tyrant. It is precisely for this reason that the teacher must devise stratagems to make himself more feared than any young rival; if he does not, he loses the best part of the class. It is my sad duty to inform the teacher that he cannot usually win over the mobile majority with acts of kindness, unless they are the sparingly used complement to acts of terror – as we will shortly see in the case of William the Conqueror. The teacher will be much consoled, however, to learn that he will not be despised by the scholar for the weight of his authority alone.

'D'you know, sir, you've made rather a hit with the fifth form?'

He and Paul were seated in the organ-loft of the village church. It was their second music-lesson.

'For goodness' sake, leave the organ alone. How d'you mean "hit"?'

'Well, Clutterbuck was in matron's room this morning. He'd just got a tin of pineapple chunks. Tangent said, "Are you going to take that into Hall?" and he said, "No, I'm going to eat it in Mr Pennyfeather's hour." "Oh no, you're not," said Tangent. "Sweets are one thing, but pineapple chunks are going too far. It's little stinkers like you," he said, "who turn decent masters savage."'

Evelyn Waugh, *Decline and Fall*

The fact that on his first day he had threatened very nearly to kill Clutterbuck with a stick seems to have done little to prevent Mr Pennyfeather from being regarded as a decent fellow.

The teacher will, though, be despised if the mobile majority considers him to have allowed his authority to fall into the wrong hands. The classroom is a frightening and lonely place for the teacher who neglects, or is unable, to exert the required amount of fear to win the many and subdue the few – for he suffers the double ignomiy of being simultaneously ridiculed and hated.

The teacher who wishes to gauge his position in this fearsome struggle may do so by considering the number of tales that he is told by sycophantic pupils. Although the teacher will of course visit the proper quantity of disdain upon the petty tell-tale, secretly he will warmly accept this act of tribute to, and confirmation of, his authority. But woe to the informant that ill reckons where the greatest danger lies, and who tells tales to a teacher whose potency is less than that of a wayward scholar.

And even the commentator who has put his faith in the virtue of nature must own that as it is with humanity, so is it also in the animal kingdom.

> We also had three golden pheasants, a cock and two hens. Nothing remarkable about that, except that when they were nine years old the cock died. Shortly afterwards one of the hens started to develop male plumage, 'crow' like a male and chase the other hen around. This metamorphosis was monitored by a great friend of my father's, John Norman, from South Kensington Natural History Museum. The complete sex change took between nine and ten months, at the end of which time it was impossible to see any variation from a normal male's plumage.
>
> **Michael Twist,** *The Spacious Days*

In all kinds of life, it would appear, there is ever one party convinced that he has been ordained to effect the oppression of another. Chickens and children alike are far more content to submit to oppression that comes from above than that which comes from their own.

It takes just one wayward scholar to expose and render foolish the teacher who, either through stratagems of his own devising, or those made available to him by senior colleagues, is unable to inspire a sufficient quantity of fear in his scholars. Since the outlawing of the various implements of correction, the teacher has become physically benign, and now has to depend a great deal on psychology:

'Why is Mr Andrews doing his bus duty with a yellow swimming hat on his head?' asked the one.

'I don't know. You'll have to ask him that,' replied the other.

He never was asked, but if he had been he would have favoured the enquirer with one of his favourite dictums: 'Every class must have its fool: if it's me, it won't have to be one of them.' It is good policy for the teacher to localise children's ridicule around areas of his own invention. The teacher who appears to be unencumbered by a sense of shame is a considerable adversary to the wayward scholar; for he ever carries with him the potential to embarrass at will. For this alone he is understood by his pupils to be dangerous.

I am dangerous, and I may do you some harm: this is the myth that the teacher must sell; and it is fear, however it is manufactured, that compels the young scholar to enter into the bargain.

The teacher is very much like the governor of a tiny kingdom, and the feudal system of submission in return for protection – upon which the harmony of the class-room state rests – is both a blessing and a curse for its scholastic subjects. The following commentary on feu-dalism is purely historical, and yet it lends itself well to the classroom:

> Its hierarchy is both intimidating and reassuring, and while the leader may operate on the basis of fear, he scares his followers less than the alternatives in a lawless and chaotic environment.

Robert Lacey and Danny Danziger, *The Year 1000: What life was like at the turn of the first millennium*

It is precisely this 'lawless and chaotic environment' that the steady scholar fears so greatly; for in such an atmosphere tyranny might, without warning, take almost any form.

I must keep my brocken chair setrish under control.
I must keep my brochen chair setrish under control.
I must keep my brocken chair setrish under control.
I must keep my brocken choir setrish under control.

I said to tom that he was a bitch and an ass because he was saying to me to go in the other group, and not stay in the group I was in

The teacher should aim to reign over his classroom like a dread sovereign: sometimes with terrible and awesome justice; sometimes with majestic leniency. When the city of Exeter dared to resist the advance of William the

Conqueror's army he attempted to change their minds by tearing out the eyes of some hostages in front of the city walls. When this failed to make the Exonians open their gates, a siege ensued. During the next eighteen days William lost half of his army. When the Exonians finally surrendered, they must have expected the worst from a man who once chopped off the right hand and left foot of 32 citizens of Alençon who had publicly taunted him about his illegitimacy. William, however, was anything but predictable in his moods. Brutal most of the time, he was also capable of acting with uncommon kindness and mercy to those who won his respect. In the vigorous defence of their city the people of Exeter had impressed William, and they were spared their lives and property. Politically it was a shrewd move, because in 1068, when the Cornish rebelled, William found loyal support amongst the people of Exeter. Moments of mercy, if used as an infrequent complement to punishment, and not as an alternative, will win the teacher loyalty and support from unexpected quarters. While the teacher might not always opt to rip out the eyes of the wayward scholar, if he wishes to be feared he must practise unpredictability.

'I know you went to Colonel Dabney's covers because you were invited. I'm not even going to send the sergeant with a note to ask if your statement is true; because I am convinced that, on this occasion, you have strictly adhered to the truth. I know, too, that you were not drinking. (You

can take off that virtuous expression, M'Turk, or I shall
begin to fear that you don't understand me.) There is not a
flaw in any of your characters. And that is why I am going
to perpetrate a howling injustice…well, now I am going to
lick you.'

Six apiece was their portion upon that word.

'And this, I think' – the head replaced the cane, and
flung the written charge into the wastepaper basket
– 'covers the situation. When you find a variation from
the normal – this will be useful to you in later life – always
meet him in an abnormal way. And that reminds me. There
are a pile of paperbacks on that shelf. You can borrow them
if you put them back. I don't think they'll take any harm
from being read in the open. They smell of tobacco, rather.
You will go to prep this evening as usual. Goodnight,' said
that amazing man.

'Goodnight, and thank you, sir.'

'I swear I'll pray for the head tonight,' said Beetle.

Rudyard Kipling, *Stalky & Co.*

That headmaster knew that Stalky & Co. had master-
minded the mischief, but he also knew that all of the
evidence available pointed to their innocence; so he told
them that he knew they were innocent according to the
letter of the law, admitted his guilt at the injustice to come,
and then committed the said injustice in the spirit, if not
the letter, of the law. Brilliant of its time, though perhaps
not to be attempted today, for, thrashings aside, the loan

of a paperback is unlikely to bring the modern scholar to his knees in thankful prayer.

Uncertainty, in the hands of a wise and authoritative ruler, gives rise to a particularly effective kind of fear. If the scholar knows exactly what is coming, the teacher is predictable; if the teacher is predictable then the pupil has less to fear. A scholar – particularly a wayward one – can easily prepare himself for almost any known rebuke: shouting; sarcasm; taunting; a stern lecturing; a 'You've let me down' talk; or being sent to his head of house – again. Such measures become enfeebled when overused. But fear of the unknown has a greater effect on modifying behaviour than admonishments the severity of which are already understood. The teacher who deals in what appears to be a random fashion generates in his pupils a fear of the uncertain, and is able to command good discipline without being considered rigid and overbearing.

In *A Book of Five Rings* revered seventeenth-century samurai Miyamoto Musashi exhorts he who would learn the Way of the Samurai to 'Attack in an unsuspected manner…Take advantage of the enemy's rhythm when he is unsettled and you can win.'

It is my recommendation that every teacher should have in his armoury a 'slower ball' – something to help him to attack in an unsuspected manner, something to cultivate a little fear. The term 'slower ball' in cricket refers to a ball bowled deceptively slowly, tricking the batsman into misplaying the shot. The bowler secretly spreads his fingers around the ball, turning his arm over at full speed when bowling. Because less of the bowler's hand is propelling the ball forward – due to the spreading of the fingers – the ball travels slightly slower than the arm speed would indicate. The batsman sees the fast arm action and plays his stroke too early, offering an easy catch or having his stumps scattered. The trick of the slower ball is that it must be used sparingly – it has to be a surprise; when every ball is a slower one, the batsman soon adjusts his stroke and scores easy runs.

If the teacher has only one delivery, the scholar will soon work him out. The teacher who always shouts, always sends the boy out, or always issues a detention would be well advised to develop a slower ball – something to cause doubt and uncertainty in the mind of the child, something to unsettle the wayward.

Miss Flavell presumes – quite correctly it transpires – that she will not be detected if she enters my class and takes a seat; after all, she has friends in my class and this will be funny to them and make her popular. Going unnoticed, however, she is forced – with no small amount of glee and self-satisfaction – to discover herself to me. She seems to expect that, upon her discovering herself, I will immediately send her back to her correct teacher with a vague and insubstantial telling off; I am, after all, busy teaching a lesson. Knowing, however, that she is expecting just this, I politely decline her offer to return to her rightful class, saying that I will not hear of her leaving so soon. Miss Flavell is at this juncture visibly and wonderfully struck by the revelation that she has lost control of her own joke, with the additional and unhappy corollary that it is now my joke. I keep her for the rest of the lesson, and most of the following break too, which, if I remember correctly, begins with lines, moves onto a recital of nursery rhymes, and ends with an explanation of the historicity of Humpty Dumpty – something, I am pleased to inform the reader, that she remembers to this day.

Mr Andrews is not my teacher
Mr Andrews is not my teacher
Mr Andrews is not my teacher
Mr Andrews is not my teacher

By having kept Miss Flavell in my lesson, retaining the ability to send her back at my pleasure, I effectively controlled for how long she would be seen to have bunked off, and, therefore, how much trouble she could expect to be in with her real teacher. Thus, by employing a non-standard response was I able to increase the level of discomfort for each successive minute that Miss Flavell remained with me, thereby mitigating against a spate of such intrusions.

With time and practice comes the confidence to bowl one's slower balls with greater daring and variety, and the ability to cause tremendous uncertainty in the mind of the wayward scholar.

Once again a double lesson after lunch on a Friday afternoon had culminated in nice boys doing silly things. I might have been more strict but, not wishing to do myself out of some end-of-the-week sport, I rode with most of it, and even encouraged some myself. Mr Marston's and Mr Davidson's glue-stick duel, however, really was a bit much; the situation being in need of some particular attention, I kept them back at the end of the lesson. Likeable scholars both, I, having no idea of how I was about to proceed, suddenly conceived the notion that if each of the boys had such a desire to daub the other in glue, I would give them a further opportunity to purge this perversion from their young minds: I would offer up my nose to them as a glue sacrifice. And so I did. And yet despite their former devotion to this branch of philosophy, my very earnest entreaties, and two almost-brand-new glue sticks, neither of them could be persuaded to daub me on the nose with sticky, and embrace me as one of their own. In fact, I was very much surprised that even when I took the lids from the glue sticks, pressed them into their hands, and presented my nose at a convenient height, the sole response of these two princes of folly was to appear embarrassed to the point of discomfort.

Despite the absurd episode having been entirely spontaneous, it had a remarkable effect in sobering the young scholars; for when I eventually desisted in my entreaties and told the boys to go for their buses, each offered an unsolicited apology – not as common as you might think. Furthermore, the genuineness of those apologies was confirmed when Mr Marston informed me that he would no longer be sitting next to his fellow glue-jouster: words he stuck by – pardon the pun – all his remaining days under my tutelage.

Sometimes an unpredictable reaction leads to an unpredictable outcome, such as the occasion on which Mr Bowden cried to his mother over the phone. He had failed to do his homework, again, and I, worrying that his condition might become contagious and he terminally ill, marched him from his classmates to a phone.
'Explain to whosoever answers that phone why it is that you are calling home at this unlikely time of day, and who it is that is standing next to you,' quoth I. I was certainly not expecting such a lachrymal spectacle, but took it – quite correctly as it turned out – to be a sign of genuine contrition. Fortunately I was able quickly to fetch The Cry Bottle from my room, and as a result of my quick thinking very few tears were lost.

MR ANDREWS CHILDREN'S TEARS

Another example of an unusual response leading to an unexpectedly advantageous outcome featured in the case of Miss Davis, who arrived at my door dripping wet, complaining that Mr Collins – a scholar not noted for the steadiness of his character – had performed an aquatic assault on her. A light investigation satisfied me that this was in fact the case, so I fetched a jug, a cup and some water from the tea room next door, and asked Miss Davis to measure out the quantity of water that she considered herself to have been abused with. I then asked Mr Collins if he thought this to be the correct amount, which, to my slight surprise, he confirmed without negotiation. These things done, I announced that at the end of the lesson we would all go outside and observe something called retribution. As the time for retribution grew nearer, so did my discomfort, for goings on such as these can culminate in an uncomfortable interview with the head. However, at the appointed time, to my great surprise and her eternal credit, Miss Davis announced that she did not wish to see Mr Collins treated as she herself had been treated, and in so doing gave a priceless and beautiful demonstration of what it is to forgive. So shines a good deed in a naughty world. One tiny tear rolled down my cheek and into a carefully positioned Cry Bottle.

But the most beautiful and enigmatic of all slower balls must surely be The Punishment Withheld – the will-o'-the-wisp of discipline.

He much regretted that his *first* tutor was dead; for whom he seemed to retain the greatest regard. He said, 'I once had been a whole morning sliding in Christ-Church meadows, and missed his lecture in logick. After dinner he sent for me to his room. I expected a sharp rebuke for my idleness, and went with a beating heart. When we were seated, he told me he had sent for me to drink a glass of wine with him, and to tell me, he was *not* angry with me for missing his lecture. This was, in fact, a most severe reprimand.'

James Boswell, *The Life of Samuel Johnson*

I have included the above examples of the slower ball not as exemplars to be followed – for this would be a treacherous pursuit – but merely as a stimulus to thought on the usefulness of uncertainty in the struggle for power within the classroom; for, while it is true that it is the certainty and not the severity of a punishment that matters most to disciplinary efficacy, it does not hold true that a particular response is the only response to any given misdemeanour. While a rational response will certainly be most commonly employed, an irrational response will often work at least as well, but with a rippling effect that travels far wider than the miscreant and the scene of his miscreancy.

The slower ball is one of the greatest celebrations of the teacher's craft, working best with foolish boys and low-level disruption – but it must be used sparingly. Once seen, the wayward scholar will develop ways to play the slower ball, so the teacher must ever be at pains to disguise and vary its delivery. There is no limit to the level of absurdity to which the teacher can descend when devising his slower balls, as the best response to well-intended, low- to mid-level miscreancy is often something less predictable. The scholastic rogue will often consider it a compliment that his teacher has taken the trouble to apply creativity to his disciplining of him, and will repay his teacher with an improved level of foolishness in the future. The slower ball is also, of course, a great comforter to the mobile majority, who are both justified and assured by it. The teacher, however, should always be humble and professional in his slower balls; for showmanship and a truly effective slower ball are almost entirely incompatible.

If all of this talk about uncertainty, power and fear appears to be misplaced and cruel, then we need to remember that, ultimately, these are acts of kindness. It has been said that a child does not have to be taught to be naughty – a truism I have well noted in the behaviours of my young niece and nephew. Indeed, the Bible remarks that folly – which has connotations far more to do with wickedness than those suggested by simple rustic foolishness – is bound up in the heart of the child. It goes on to say that the means to drive that folly out is the rod of discipline. Discipline, however, I will attend to in the following chapter; for you will note that fear – the threat of being disciplined – is that which might save the child from requiring the rod in the first instance, and so must come first in the order of things.

For most young scholars naughtiness is an innate quality – a built-in response and a rebellious challenge to the authority of adults. Most of us, regardless of age, would agree that behaving badly can be very appealing; but unfortunately for the scholar, bad behaviour often leads to punishment. This leaves the scholar facing a dilemma that he finds impossible to reconcile: misbehaviour is irresistible but punishment is painful. He longs for somebody to take this difficult decision out of his hands, for the teacher who forces him to behave in such a way as to keep him out of the trouble that it is incumbent upon him to get himself into: he longs for someone to fear. The age at which the wayward scholar may become aware that he harbours such feelings is around the same age as he begins to appreciate the efforts of his parents: thirty, give or take a decade. This is the approximate age at which often begins the affectionate reminiscence of strict teachers. Please do not confuse strict with mean: nobody has fond recollections of the petty, mood-driven child-hater, with his inconsistencies and sickly attempts to be liked. Equating strictness to a consistent and insistent approach to high standards, the strict teacher helps to keep the potentially errant scholar from the ever-gaping jaws of punishment; for when the scholar is not sure what he is allowed to get away with he will invariably attempt to get away with more than he can. My own experience of punishment, though naturally limited, is that it is seldom fun; so when the once wayward scholar reflects on his schooling, it is often the teachers who kept him out of trouble that he has the highest regard for. It is possible for the teacher to be highly regarded by the wayward scholar purely because the former exerts sufficient fear and authority over the latter to keep him from the pain of punishment.

And so, then, we come on to the issue of shouting. Those of you who note that shouting is a form of discipline, and as such should be reserved for the final chapter, are not without a valid point; however, shouting is also a means to creating the kind of fear from which good things might spring. We tend to think that nothing good can come from fear, and yet this is not so. Consider the case of Mr Mayor.

Mr Mayor, I am reliably informed by one who was there, shouted so terrifyingly at a class of eleven-year-olds that even the teacher taking their lesson cried. Their crime? They had trodden mud into the classroom in which he was about to teach. His lambaste so affected the tender scholars of this class that, come September, cheers were sung by all who had escaped his tutelage: a complete and utter fear of him haunted them for all their remaining days at that establishment. Misbehaving in Mr Mayor's lesson was something that simply did not happen, and the reason for this was fear.

Upon first hearing of this I was shocked by the ferocity of this man, and appalled by this abuse of power in a position of tremendous influence. There is, however, a different way of looking at the behaviour of Mr Mayor on that day. How many children were spared the pains of discipline for fear of this man? How many punishments, detentions, suspensions and expulsions were rendered unnecessary through his fearsome reputation? How much more homework completed? How much less messing about indulged in? We can never know; and yet, as unlikely as it may sound, his violent eruption on that day may have been the result of careful consideration, of deep vision. Is it possible that you, like I, have kicked a bin in unbridled fury while smiling on the hidden side of your face? We are actors! The whole display might very well have been a contrived and controlled spectacle of outward emotion over something that, in reality, bothered him little: perhaps, that is, he had no real appetite for power but, realising that somebody had to have it, and noting the absence of anyone more suitably qualified, concluded that the burden must fall on him. I am not saying that this was definitely the case, but neither can anybody else say that it definitely was not. The difference between genuine rage and a controlled explosion is often not appreciated by those looking on, and it is a brave and visionary teacher who is willing to sacrifice the short-term approval of parents, colleagues and children in order to affect long-term improvements – improvements that will bring no thanks but much progress. We allow our doctors to make dramatic, shocking, yet ultimately unprovable claims to instigate potentially life-saving changes in the behaviour of their patients; the same licence should be extended to the teacher, and this may include the use of a raised voice.

The teacher may be fortunate to work in a school where the necessary dose of fear is held in the hands of just one or two senior persons, thereby allowing the teacher to go about his daily business in a genial manner, enjoying all the benefits of the latent and vicarious fearsomeness attached to him. What is more probably the case, however, is that he cannot rely on other people's fear nowadays; he has to create his own.

Those who denounce the brutality of shouting often do so to obscure any contemplation of the emotional brutality that we now seem to favour. In times past a boy would have undergone the tyranny of a thick ear, whereas now he is told that he has let down his school, his teacher, his parents, his friends; but is the second any less tyrannous than the first? The emotional torture that we so congratulate ourselves in administering in place of that which affects the body is to some wayward scholars far more hurtful than the unself-righteous tap of the cane ever was, and may even do more lasting damage. I will not discourse on corporal punishment here, that being a subject I want to reserve for my final chapter; I wish only to make the point that shouting is not inherently wicked, and is, in some cases, a lot less tyrannous than a protracted bout of emotional torture. But if the teacher must shout, there is no need for him to be abusive.

> We ought never to allow our instincts of justice to degenerate into mere vindictiveness.
>
> **Jerome K. Jerome,** *Three Men in a Boat*

Somewhat paradoxically, I feel it necessary at this point to say that shouting and strong discipline do not generally exhibit a positive correlation. More often than not the one is inversely proportional to the other, and this is born out in the observable fact that the weak teacher, nine times out of ten, shouts more than the strict teacher. Furthermore, while there certainly is such a thing as righteous anger, anger *per se* is not a trait that we need to teach to our scholars (except on special occasions); it is an emotion to which they will be more than adequately exposed even without the teacher's demonstrations. And does not the book of Proverbs warn, 'A fool uttereth all his mind: but a wise man keepeth it in till afterwards' (29:11).

No, I am quite certain that a particular circumstance brought about through quiet expectation commands far more authority – and is that not what the teacher needs most? – than a spitting, a reddening, a stammering, a bulging of the veins at the temples.

Therefore, when the scholars were making a very bad job of lining up outside my classroom, I disappeared into my room and returned with a three-foot rule which, having affected phlegm, I proceeded gently to offer up against the remnant. This simple and silent act was enough to encourage most of the ragged column to reverence the wall with their shoulders, whispering their colleagues into a like propriety. The outstanding minority, shamed by conspicuity, quickly arranged themselves in accordance with their classmates, whereupon I offered some thoughts on the menace that can issue from unkempt lines. Line-forming, like many things in education, is best achieved through the manipulation of the scholar against his own. The teacher must consider that far less energy is required of him when children line up because they are expected to, rather than because he has raised his voice and told them to. There is also something deeply troubling in the teacher having to ask for something which, if he be properly feared, ought to be his by right: for to draw attention to the lack of that which ought to be obtained through expectation alone, is for the teacher to make an advertisement of a disciplinary slight.

I beg the reader's permission to make a not entirely unwarranted digression on the theme of patience versus tolerance – for it is at such times as wrath is in the ascendant that such a timely reflection may prove profitable.

We often use the terms tolerance and patience inter-changeably, but there is a notable difference between the two. To tolerate another you do not have to agree with him; nor do you have to like him; you simply allow him to exist without comment from you; you peacefully coexist with him; you respect his personal choices and you refrain from imposing your personal choices on him. However, there happen in schools a great many despicable things that ought not to be tolerated at all, but which the teacher is powerless to stop – such as penlessness. What, then, should the teacher do? Tolerate things that he knows to be wrong, or admit his impotence? I believe that it is better to view such atrocities from a position of patience rather than tolerance: 'Your not having a pen is wrong; I am not going to tolerate it; it is not all right. I am going to wait patiently for the day when you arrive with a pen, without ever condoning your current penless state. I may wait for weeks, I may wait for years, I may wait in vain, but I will exercise patience over tolerance; for it is far better for me to wait patiently for the day when you arrive with a writing implement, and for you to know and understand why I am waiting, than it is for you to mis-guidedly believe that I am tolerating your penlessness.' By substituting, in place of the pen, the peculiarities of his own misfortunes, I hope the reader will now begin to see that there is more fulfilment to be found in looking patiently to-wards the day of rectitude, no matter how distant-seeming, than in blithely tolerating the evil of the dark day at hand.

Let us return once more to the subject of shouting, and, more particularly, to its several associated problems; for, if shouting be poorly used, it can result in the creation of problems far more acute than those it was first employed to solve. I would like to make five points regarding the problem of shouting.

1 If you bark or snap, you lose them. That's what they get from parents and the schools in general, the bark and the snap. If they strike back with the silent treatment, you're finished in the classroom…They know it's a forty-minute showdown, you versus them.

Frank McCourt, *Teacher Man*

If they do not turn against the teacher with all their collective or solitary might, they will probably retreat into a sullen, brooding place from which he may never again draw them. For those who must stand at the front of a class, the second of these two extremes is, in my opinion, the less pleasant; for children are experts at this kind of warfare.

Garden Minimus played his small part in the whole affair by being sulky and obstinate during the whole of first hour. It was a game that he was perfectly accustomed to playing, and he knew every move from the opening gambit of 'saying things under your breath that looked bad but couldn't possibly be heard,' to the triumphant checkmate of a studied, sarcastic politeness that was most unusual and hinted at danger.

Hugh Walpole, *Mr Perrin and Mr Traill*

2 Shouting can lead to long-term alienation between teacher and scholar; for it is in such moments of lucid anger that the one most runs the risk of telling the other exactly what he thinks of him. A whole class can be lost forever in one outburst of honest invective, and here I speak from painful experience. While the teacher may presume that upon hearing the unpleasant truth about their behaviour or prospects a class or individual will be transported into reformation, this is, unfortunately, almost never the case.

> If you tell me I am a scoundrel I may mend my ways, but if you tell me I am a eunuch you are tempting me to hit back in any way that seems feasible. If you want to make an enemy of a man tell him that his ills are incurable.

George Orwell, *The Road to Wigan Pier*

It is a grave mistake for the teacher to tell even the very wayward scholar that his ills are incurable (or, for that matter, that he is a eunuch); it almost never has the desired effect. He rarely agrees with his teacher, who then has to live with the irrevocable consequences of his honest appraisal for as long as both parties continue at the school. Yet there is another more momentous reason for the teacher to resist all temptation to supply his honest appraisal to even the most rancid youth, and, in expressing this point, I will not attempt to improve on the words of C.S. Lewis.

This same spiritual law works terribly in the opposite direction. The Germans, perhaps, at first ill-treated the Jews because they hated them: afterwards they hated them much more because they had ill-treated them. The more cruel you are, the more you will hate; and the more you hate, the more cruel you will become – and so on in a vicious circle for ever. Good and evil both increase at compound interest. That is why the little decisions that you and I make every day are of such infinite importance.

C.S. Lewis, *Mere Christianity*

The teacher is very likely to be wondering how to go about cultivating these noble feelings towards those scholars that he would much prefer to drag around by the ear. The answer is not for him to feel, but to act. The teacher must act as if dragging him around by the ear were the very last thing that he wished to do to him – for in showing kindness to the undeserving the teacher heaps hot coals on the head of his adversary, not all of which will go unnoticed. It is futile for the teacher to sit about trying to manufacture feelings of love for someone whom he despises; he must act in a manner the very reverse of human nature and wait for the compound interest to roll in. C.S. Lewis again: 'Very often the only way to get a quality in reality is to start behaving as if you had it already.' Or, as Hamlet said, 'Assume a virtue, if you have it not.'

There will be occasions, however, when the teacher will simply need to get the wayward scholar out of his

'Mr Evans, you and I need some time apart, with a door between us. Since the law requires me to remain in this classroom, with these, your classmates, it is you who must leave.'

sight before the former falls over Bellow Brink and risks incurring some of the pitfalls therewith associated. The scholar – even the culpable one – is fairly understanding on such occasions, and would generally rather spend a few minutes alone in the corridor than undergo a public lambasting. With this in mind, the teacher may wish to send him out with an egg timer and an instruction to return when the sands of time indicate. The egg timer has a wonderful way of simultaneously saying both 'Get out!' and 'Come back'. There will always be, however, those scholars for whom an hour glass will be hardly sufficient.

3 Once the teacher has shouted as loud as he can (I am not talking about a raised yet measured voice) he has nothing left in reserve. One tiny smirk from the wayward scholar will expose the fragility of his position and the teacher will have nothing left to counter with. The teacher who maintains his equanimity can always at least counter with a public display of having not been being particularly moved, and the teacher who refrains from shouting always appears to have something in reserve, which, even if it never be used, is in itself a position of strength. Samurai Musashi wrote wisely of strategy when he advised, 'An elevated spirit is weak and a low spirit is weak. Do not let the enemy see your spirit.'

4 It is not the classroom teacher's job to get angry; the teacher's job in this respect is merely to fulfil his role in the system of justice that operates within his school. Ultimately, the severity of an offence will not be seen in the loudness of shouting but in the gravity of the penalty. Since the teacher often does not decide the ultimate sanction for an offence, he must proceed with caution; for it would be a bad thing if he were to make a great deal of something that those in positions above him, either through inclination or incompetence, treated as trifling. The only person who might be entitled to demonstrate his anger audibly at a misdemeanour is that person who will exact the penalty; for only they can know if the penalty to be invoked will be commensurate to a display of wrath. Ironically, however, this person is the least likely to give voice to his anger, because he is able to communicate his displeasure through the severity of his penalty; hence the

sobriety of judges. Therefore, let classroom teachers do their jobs, and headteachers do theirs.

5 Finally, on the problem of shouting, it is difficult enough to deliver an admonition without fluffing one's lines, even without shouting.

I was Mucking About in Class

I was mucking about in class
Mr Brown said,
Get out and take your chair with me
I suppose he meant to say
Take your chair with you
So Dave said,
Yeah – you heard what he said
get out and take my chair with him
so Ken said,
Yeah – get out and take his chair with me
So I said to Mr Brown
Yessir – shall I take our chair with you, sir?
Wow
that meant BIG TROUBLE

Michael Rosen

Emotion in excess never did kind things for clarity of diction, and the teacher must ever be mindful that the point of maximum terror is very close to the point of maximum comedy. The teacher must consider this carefully.

Discipline

Whoso loveth instruction loveth knowledge: but he that hateth reproof is brutish.

Proverbs 12:1

In this final chapter the noble purpose of discipline will be discussed, particularly in so much as it is a charitable act done out of kindness – for the one who disciplines seldom gains much, if anything at all, by so doing. The necessity of pain in discipline will be studied, and there will be a short discourse on corporal punishment. The teacher will then be warned against the hazards of striving to be liked, and the danger of attempting to see the harvest of his labours ere young John Barleycorn has grown a beard. This final chapter will close with an offering to the teacher of some practical advice along the theme of things to try and things not to try.

The very first piece of advice that was given to me as a young man when I joined the teaching profession was from a headmaster, who invested me with the following piece of wisdom: the discipline is in the subject. He went on to reveal that if children behaved badly, it was because the lesson was too difficult, too simple or too dull. The perfect lesson for the occasion, he maintained, would produce the perfect behaviour. I believed him, and made a solemn vow to ensure that my lessons were all things to all children, banishing from my classroom both indiscipline and all of its attendant disciplinary requirements; and if I did discover myself issuing reproofs, I would find the fault in my teaching and remedy my shortcomings by the next lesson.

I often wish that what that venerable man had told me was the truth – teaching would be so much easier, yet possibly less entertaining, if the behaviour of children was so predictable and simple to control. Experience, though, that great master of learning, has taught me otherwise. I can now see that this noble ideal has no place in the volatile world of classroom education. For I have, albeit only once or twice, taken a well planned and interesting lesson, and set it before a class of unruly children: did they suddenly and immediately learn how to behave? Did they take their pens from their adversaries' foreheads and unleash them on their exercise books? Did they desist from abusing one another and enter into a deep contemplation of my lesson objective? No they did not! I cast my pearls before swine, who, after they had trampled them into the ground, turned on me. Those who believe that a passionate exposition of the subject is automatically enough to command good discipline in wayward scholars have an optimism which is to be envied. Discipline must come before education, because without discipline, education is compromised: a lack of discipline reduces one's capacity to learn. Rather than discipline being revealed through the subject, may I suggest that the subject is revealed through discipline. It is precisely for this reason that every good teacher must be a disciplinarian, no matter how little he likes the title.

A good teacher is a determined person. This was widely known in the nineteenth century. That was a time of strong-willed parents and tough teachers. Sometimes they were merely tyrants. But sometimes they were wise, firm, and efficient educators: and even if the children they produced did often rebel, they became well-educated rebels…Still, it seems that some teachers do not know why they must have a strong will and exercise it: they are perhaps a little ashamed of the necessity, even afraid of it; they feel that in a perfect society no display of will-power would be needed in the schools. But it would.

Consider how many different kinds of resistance the teacher has to overcome. To begin with, the young do not like work. They would rather be playing football, or sitting in the movies eating popcorn. But they must learn to work, because they will assuredly have to work all the rest of their lives; and to teach them that work is unnecessary or avoidable is to deform their characters…Nor do the young like authority. They are natural anarchists. They would prefer a world of unpredictable disorder, without duties or responsibilities. Such a world is impracticable now. So the young must be taught to respect the principle of authority; and if they do not learn it in school they will find it very bitter to learn later…Also the young hate concentration. It is an effort, an unfamiliar and painful effort.

Gilbert Highet, *The Art of Teaching*

The purpose of education is to improve people; discipline is the foremost practical application of this improvement process. Discipline is done to people that you love or care deeply for because you want to see them better themselves and their situation.

As many as I love, I rebuke and chasten.

Revelation 3:19

Discipline is an emotive word that is all too easily attached to antiquated images of dusty schoolrooms and canings, but the word must be denuded of this ancient imagery if we are to understand its role as the eternal agent of improvement. Discipline has to be the cornerstone of any improvement process because without some measure of discomfort an individual is unlikely to change his behaviour radically. It is precisely for this reason that Aristotle wrote, 'We cannot learn without pain.'

Homework Homework Homework Homework Homework Homework
Homework Homework Homework Homework Homework
Homework Homework Homework Homework Homework Homework...
homework Homework Homework Homework homework homework

The pain may be emotional or physical, but without it there is no discomfort to direct the child towards improvement. Often, the seemingly unnecessary discomfort administered to a child during disciplining is intended as a tiny replica of the adult anguish that he can expect to inherit if he does not alter his behaviour or attitude. Discipline is a valiant attempt to change for the better the lifelong journey of the wayward child. Softly, softly, and an inexhaustible supply of last chances may make the teacher feel nice and charitable, but will help the child only in becoming increasingly hard to improve. The improvement of wilful boys and girls occurs only once the painful consequences of doing something wrong becomes greater than the discomfort of making the required changes; thus, it can be seen that any disciplinary measure that is not adequately painful will not work. One has only to look at the weekly detention list and see the same scholars being punished for the same offences, week after week, to realise that detentions, by themselves – unless of exceptional quality – are insufficiently painful.

Just such an example of an exceptional detention did I witness when visiting a school in South Africa. A boy who had with some cockiness refused the instruction of a prefect – thereby challenging the authority of the head himself – was spending his lunchtime on 'Reflection', an uncomplicated business which required him to stand in front of a wall for one hour, encouraged, one presumes, to reflect on his conduct. Now I defy even the most torpid of observers to contend that the hapless object of this piece of discipline could pass an entire week's lunchtimes in such a manner without developing a distinct sense of having been disciplined. Although all discipline intends improvement, or at least ought to, it is unfortunate for the majority of us that this same improvement is engendered by something altogether more brutal, and for which we are not usually thankful.

'Thank you, Sir, I deserve the chastisement your words give me.'

Now no chastening for the present seemeth to be joyous, but grievous: nevertheless afterward it yieldeth the peaceable fruit of righteousness unto them which are exercised thereby.

Hebrews 12:11

Whosoever makes discipline the cornerstone of his teaching will find the greater part of his work already done; but the teacher who depends on maths, history or French to discipline his pupils organically on the basis that his love of the subject will be echoed by the young scholar deludes himself wildly: for the teacher often forgets that he teaches children with aspirations quite different to, and sometimes rather lower than, his own. The teacher who loves his subject, holds it to be intrinsically important, and wants to encourage others to the same belief, would be well advised to put discipline on at least a level footing with technique. With discipline as the foundation stone of the classroom, the teacher at least has the opportunity to state the case for the lesson and win some children for his subject; this almost never happens in the midst of chaotic behaviour. And we must also acknowledge that it is not just the education of those who are deserving of chastisement that suffers when discipline is either spared or ineffectual, but the education of the well-behaved too; for, as already noted in the previous chapter, a room where indiscipline reigns is not a safe place for the steady scholar to be.

I must not knee Josh in the Groin
I must not knee Josh in the groin
I. must not knee Josh in the Groin
I must not knee Josh in the groin

Discipline has long been seen by some as an unnecessary nastiness delivered by megalomaniacs into the lives of cherubs, and has become a vulgar word to our many graduates of those ever-thriving establishments The School of Political Correctness and The College of Doing Good. Euphemisms such as 'behaviour management' now convey the notion that there is no such thing as bad behaviour, just behaviour that needs to be managed. Actions that were once palpably wrong are now merely inappropriate, and the result of poor decision-making. The prevalent theory seems to be that if we simply help children to see themselves as decision-makers, they will act rationally and responsibly, and make the right decisions for themselves and those around them. Yet even where 99 children in 100 justify this faith in youth, the poor decisions of the one will still render miserable the lives of the rest. Yes, the wayward scholar's decision to throw a chair across the room does make for a poor decision, a very poor one indeed; but it is

'And there's another poor decision for you.'

particularly poor for the scholar who sits at the end of its trajectory. Referring to the scholar who does such things as a poor decision-maker is, I suggest, to gild the pig's ear.

Much is said about the rights of the child, but what the child really needs are not rights, but protection: protection from himself and protection from others. The scholar has not lived long enough, or diversely enough, to know what is beneficial for himself; he knows what he wants – things that might seem good or pleasing to him in the short term, but he knows little of what is good for him in the long term. The most important lessons that are taught in schools are long-term lessons that often take many years to hit their mark, lessons such as obedience being an everyday part of adult and working life. The teacher who hands the wayward scholar over to his own whims and tastes is a scoundrel not worthy of the position he holds. The pupil in his care grows up to become an adult who knows his desires and his rights, but who wields them clumsily, and with little regard for his responsibility to others. The analogy of a child's mind trapped in an adult's body is somewhat trite, and yet it is appropriate when I consider the way in which I have observed some parents to behave. The link between rights and responsibilities takes only a moment to point out, but a good part of a lifetime to comprehend; for responsibility is something which is produced by years of having one's indisciplined corners knocked off – a state that is necessarily lacking in the young scholar.

'I have decided that although by smashing your face in I would gain an advantage, you would not be mutually benefitted by said decision and, therefore, I will desist thereof.'

Today in schools discipline is meted out emotionally, whereas in the past it was dealt out physically. What is often overlooked, however, is that the first is not necessarily any less tyrannous than the second, any preference being more a matter of taste than morality. One might well consider the long-term implications of the softly spoken classic, 'You've let me down; you've let the school down; you've let your parents down; and you've let yourself down.' One can never know how often such speeches are replayed in the last thoughts of those who take their own lives.

In laying before the reader a second observation on the subject of physical punishment, I will leave him in the capable hands Dr Johnson and Mr Boswell, begging only that he enter into a particularly deep contemplation of the final sentences.

> Indeed Johnson was very sensible how much he owed to Mr Hunter. Mr Langton one day asked him how he had acquired so accurate a knowledge of Latin, in which, I believe, he was exceeded by no man of his time; he said, 'My master whipt me very well. Without that, Sir, I should have done nothing.' He told Mr Langton, that while Hunter was flogging his boys unmercifully, he used to say, 'And this I do to save you from the gallows.' Johnson, upon all occasions, expressed his approbation of enforcing instruction by means of the rod. 'I would rather (he said) have the rod to be the general terror to all, to make them learn, than tell a child, if you do thus, or thus, you will be more esteemed than your brothers or sisters. The rod produces an effect that terminates in itself. A child is afraid of being whipped, and gets his task, and there's an end on't; whereas, by exciting emulation and comparisons of superiority, you lay the foundation of lasting mischief; you make brothers and sisters hate each other.

> **James Boswell,** *The Life of Samuel Johnson*

But would I, in these enlightened times, advocate a return to those ancient implements of correction? No, I would not, and the reason is this: one cannot, in schools, be certain that those implements would be used with love. We know, for instance, that when the ominously named Thwackum delivered his correction to Tom Jones, with the old flogging line, 'Castigo te non quod odio habeam, sed quod Amem' – 'I chastise thee not out of hatred, but out of love' – that this Thwackum's love was very far indeed from the young Tom.

All discipline should be born out of love and a desire to generate improvement, but the past has shown us that teachers, to their lasting disgrace, have frequently devolved themselves of this responsibility, and have set a generous limitation on the boundary of their wrath.

> 'D'you get the cane?'
>
> 'It didn't hurt,' I said proudly.
>
> Flip had heard everything. Instantly her voice came screaming after me:
>
> 'Come here! Come here this instant! What was that you said?'
>
> 'I said it didn't hurt,' I faltered out.
>
> 'How dare you say a thing like that? Do you think that is the proper thing to say? Go in and REPORT YOURSELF AGAIN!'
>
> This time Sambo laid on in real earnest. He continued for a length of time that frightened and astonished me – about five minutes, it seemed – ending up by breaking the riding crop. The bone handle went flying across the room. 'Look what you made me do!' he said furiously, holding up the broken crop.
>
> **George Orwell,** *Such, Such Were the Joys*

And this because an eight-year-old Eric Blair, new to St Cyprians, had wet the boarding school bed for a fourth or fifth time.

Discipline without love becomes merely anger, aggression or revenge, the fruits of which are never pleasant to observe.

> We may kill if necessary, but we must not hate and enjoy hating. We may punish if necessary, but we must not enjoy it.
>
> **C.S. Lewis,** *Mere Christianity*

One teacher may cane the scholar with love; another may love caning the scholar. Since it is not possible to know the minds of these two ministers of discipline, the law must incline itself in such a way as to eradicate the possibility of abuse.

For the imaginative teacher, though, corporal punishment need not to have altogether disappeared. When I discovered two scholars that found great amusement in slapping each other's faces during lesson time, I provided for them at the end of my lesson an opportunity more freely to indulge this pastime. The gentlemen concerned were at first reluctant to take up my offer, so I gently informed them that I had been poetical in my employment of the word 'offer', and that they could enjoy no liberty until they had slapped each other on the face three more times apiece. Their opening exchanges were tentative and weak as they sought to identify a strategy for managing the situation without dishonouring their friendship. By their third slaps, however, they had rediscovered their erstwhile love of slapping and were joyfully trading lusty blows.

On another occasion I took a jar of extra-hot chillies into school and placed them on my desk – as an ingredient of my lunch, you will understand – knowing full well what would follow; for they were of the brightest hue of red and green, and soon caught the attention of the scholars. Despite weakly and insincerely attempting to dissuade them from such a foolish endeavour, I soon had a number of desperate show-offs (boys, naturally) who had set their tender hearts on eating one of these by now notorious chillies. I, with a great show of reluctance, selected the boy who, in my teaching of him, had given me the least cause for rejoicing. Once more I tried to dissuade him by alluding to the severity of the chillies, their cost, and the unlikelihood of him liking the taste; but a strong desire to show off has ever been the Achilles heel of the wayward scholar. Finally, I made the boy solemnly promise that he would under no circumstances spit out, and thus waste, the precious delicacy; all these conditions he far too easily and gladly assented to. I offered him the jar, and he put one in his mouth and began to chew, and – for a moment – he was enormously pleased with himself. Oh how he swelled like a cock turkey at his being the sole object of attention to a room's-worth of his own. A moment later and his schoolboy grin had exchanged itself for a rather different expression. His eyes darted around the room looking first for assurance, and then for a bin. But I stood right in front of him demanding, to the delight of everybody, that he 'Eat it, eat it!' To give the boy his due he did complete his ill-chosen feast, and, even though it was rumoured that he went home at lunchtime with 'stomach pains', I never heard any more of the matter, narrowly escaping, perhaps, an interview with the head.

A similar thing did I do along the lines of 'Does anybody want to smell something really disgusting?' but insisted that the boy – it is always a boy, this one selected because he had managed to turn his whole body into the shape of a raised arm, while shouting 'Pick me! Pick me!' – had to take a good, deep sniff – nothing tentative. Despite him visibly retching, demand flourished, and most of the boys felt obliged to take their turn.

I will give just one more example of self-administered corporal punishment concerning a Mr Newson, a quite brilliant fool – possibly the best that I have worked with. He appeared to have inexhaustible reserves of good-natured stupidity, and, had he lived some five hundred years ago, would almost certainly have worn the royal coxcomb. In this particular lesson Mr Newson was taking great delight in the manufacture of a considerable racket, through spreading his left hand on the desk and striking successive gaps between fingers with a pen, wielded with as much venom and alacrity as he dared. Naively thinking that this interference would soon go away, I did what the Romans said never to do – I postponed the war to his advantage. The noise got faster and louder and, recognising at last that something needed to be done, I reached into my desk drawer. 'If you must do that,' said I, walking to the back of the classroom and handing him a pair of compasses, 'could you at least do it with something sharp?' Now, the average corrupter of gravity would see this as the natural conclusion to an episode of annoying his teacher – not so Mr Newson. The effect was quite as if I had picked up the compasses in my own hands and stabbed him about the fingers.

The teacher that does not discipline the child – whether it is because he cannot or will not – is guilty of propelling him towards a bleak future. 'Chasten thy son while there is hope,' saith the Bible (Proverbs 19:18). A failure to discipline him while there is hope deprives him of the single thing that can bring about his improvement.

There are two considerations that the teacher need be wary of regarding the disciplining of children: firstly, that the teacher should not be too eager to be liked, and secondly, that he should not be too eager to see the fruit of his influence in the lives of those he teaches.

To address the first point, then. It would be unusual for the teacher not to want to be liked by the children he teaches, and the suitability and motivation of such a person in the teaching profession would need to be carefully considered. However, what he quietly desires and what he actively courts as a teacher with an important duty are two very different things.

> I say that a prince must want to have a reputation for compassion rather than for cruelty: none the less he must be careful that he does not make bad use of compassion... By making an example or two he will prove more compassionate than those who, being too compassionate, allow disorders that lead to murder and rapine. These nearly always harm the whole community, whereas executions ordered by a prince affect only individuals.

Niccolò Machiavelli, *The Prince*

Such was the case of the boy who, because I had kindly – and as it proved remissly – allowed him to go to the toilet without having signed The Toilet Book, disrupted another class by making unholy gestures at his friend through a window. The teacher should not be oppressive, but neither should he compromise to the point where he starts habitually to break his own rules. I am reminded of the words of *Test Match Special* scorer Bill Frindall, correcting someone for referring to the 'rules' of cricket: 'They're not rules,' he said sourly, 'they're laws. Rules can be broken, laws cannot.'

Pleasing children must never come before improving children, and, as for being liked, it is a perk, a fortunate by-product of good practice, and not something to be sought in the first instance, and above the teacher's duty.

When he had first come to Brookfield he had aimed to
be loved, honoured and obeyed – but obeyed, at any rate.
Obedience he had secured, and honour had been granted
him; but only now came love, the sudden love of boys for
a man who was kind without being soft, who understood
them well enough, but not too much, and whose private
happiness linked him with their own.

James Hilton, *Good-Bye, Mr Chips*

And, as Proverbs 28:23 informs us, 'He that rebuketh a man
afterwards shall find more favour than he that flattereth
with the tongue.' It is no coincidence, therefore, that
when grown-ups reminisce over their favourite teachers
the word 'strict' is usually amongst the first words to be
mentioned. The names of these famous men and women
are long remembered, and not without good reason; for
they had vision enough to shape and improve us at a time
when we did not want to be shaped or improved. Maths,
science, geography, French, these are not measures of
improvement, they are merely vehicles for it; for there is
very little worth measuring in schools that can actually
be measured.

Children like the teachers that they are getting a good
deal from; they like teachers who are civil, can keep them
from the mischief that it is incumbent upon them to get
into, and who can actually teach them something new or
interesting into the bargain; all of these things, no matter
how it is concealed, require a measure of discipline.

His manner was perfect: no familiarity, no hostility, no threadbare humour; mutual respect; decorum…Thus, even had he taught us nothing else, to be in Smewgy's form was to be in a measure ennobled. Amidst all the banal ambition and flashy splendours of school life he stood as a permanent reminder of things more gracious, more humane, larger and cooler. But his teaching, in the narrower sense, was equally good.

C.S. Lewis, *Surprised By Joy*

School should not be a bubble in which the realities of the world to come are deferred; instead, school ought to be a miniature replica of the real world, where the scholar can make relatively unimportant mistakes but be forcibly encouraged to learn from them. Regardless of whether the wayward scholar comes from a disadvantaged background or not, he should not be given an inexhaustible supply of chances; for this simply disadvantages him further by robbing him of the opportunity to learn from mistakes.

A man of great wrath shall suffer punishment: for if thou deliver him thou must do it again.

Proverbs 19:19

The many chances given also offer little satisfaction to the mobile majority – whose allegiance and morality is ever out to tender, leaving them highly likely to begin their own investigations into whether they too have an inexhaustible supply of chances.

Children will need to learn the lessons that life demands of us all, but it is largely adults who decide whether such lessons will be learned the hard way, the easy way, or at all. The teacher who fails to take responsibility for the discipline of the child when at school colludes, by neglect, in encouraging him along a path of deviancy, and perhaps even criminality, when he leaves.

The teacher should not aim to feel warm and cosy in his dealings with scholars. He will, of course, rejoice to see a child happy in his presence, but not if such happiness must be dearly paid for by the scholar in the days and years to come. The teacher has an educational duty to perform, and his own feelings must not be allowed to compromise this duty; he must set his mind to the silent conviction that if he follows his duty the scholar will be better prepared for the future.

A passionate teacher may be quiet and fastidious just as she may be tough and vigorous; but the pupils know about teachers who are committed to them, and forgive them a lot. Teachers may punish, berate, drive, enforce, and even once in a while be unreasonable; but the fire, the bothering, gives children a feel of security and animation: they sense that the experience is worth having.

You must care about what I do, how I behave, how I work. Such caring is signalled in a large number of small matters. It matters how you speak to me, how you mark my work, how you look at me. There is a distinctive warmth and interest in those who care – nothing phoney about it. The child makes a ruthless distinction between caring and indifference. Caring motivates. It not only makes you feel better; it makes you work better. It oils the relationships in the classroom. It enhances the way you value yourself.

Caring is not the same as kindness. It is possible to be kind but not caring.

David Winkley, *Handsworth Revolution*

Which brings me to the second point, that the teacher should not be too keen to behold the fruits of his influence.

A teacher affects eternity; he can never tell where his influence stops.

Henry B. Adams, *The Education of Henry Adams*

Who has done the world the greater service, the teacher whose teaching was enjoyed by thousands, or the teacher whose teaching was enjoyed by only a few? The answer is nobody knows. Who is to say that the unspectacular teacher did not drop a chance word deep into the soul of a previously uninspired student that set him on a voyage of discovery that benefitted millions? It is for this reason that there should be no competition amongst teachers; it will exist surely enough, but no policy should ever be promoted which would encourage it. Let every teacher say only, 'I have done my share.' For if he has done his share he has done enough; let others do theirs.

'Let us now praise famous men' –
Men of little showing –
For their work continueth,
And their work continueth,
Broad and deep continueth,
Greater than their knowing!

Rudyard Kipling, *Stalky & Co.*

The teacher should not be overly anxious to see the salutary influence of his discipline born out in the behaviour of the scholar; for efforts directed at the long-term improvement of children are often met with hostility from the very people who stand most to benefit from them. The fruit of discipline can be a long summer in the ripening; but ripen it invariably does, and the teacher who has the foresight to live in his catchment will have the pleasure of seeing at least some of that fruit, for most children turn out well enough once they begin to make their own way in life.

'It was a very trivial incident but it must have impressed me at the time. Why else would it have stayed in the mind for nearly twenty years? It concerned two boys, Petherick and "Chuff" Rogers, who accompanied me over to Barcombe by train, when we were giving a charity performance of that year's opera. It was Christmas time, of course, and the train was very full. We finally secured seats in a compartment where a young woman was nursing a baby. Within minutes of starting out the baby was dramatically sick...I remember poor Petherick's expression well, as he took refuge behind my copy of *The Times*. Upside down it was, but a thing like that wouldn't bother Petherick. He was one of our skyrockets, and went on to become president of a famous insurance company, and collect the OBE, or whatever they give the cream of insurance brokers. But I wasn't thinking so much of Petherick but of Chuff. Always unlucky, he had been sitting alongside the mother, and was thus on the receiving end of the business. I didn't know what to do but Chuff did. He whipped out a handkerchief – the only clean handkerchief I'd ever seen him sport – leaned across, wiped the baby's face and then the mother's lap. And when I say "wiped" I mean wiped. It wasn't a dab. It was more of a general tidy-up, all round. After that we had a tolerably uneventful journey, with Rogers making soothing noises all the way to the junction.

'Now some of you might think that this is a very damp squib to conclude the regular fireworks display we have had here tonight, with so many kind speeches and the giving of such splendid farewell gifts, but it isn't, you know. It's very relevant, to me at any rate, relevant to what we've all been engaged in up here on the moor all these years. For Chuff Rogers, bless his thick skull, never won a prize or a race in his life. Neither did he find time to do the only thing he was equipped to do – raise a family. He was killed at First Ypres, but I still remember him. Rather better than I remember Petherick. As a matter of fact, when I came across his name this morning, I thought of him as one of our outstanding successes.'

R.F. Delderfield, *To Serve Them All My Days*

Academic subjects provide a framework for children to be advanced both cognitively and socially, and very enjoyable they can be, too; but they are not themselves a worthwhile measure of teaching. The most noble and laudable undertakings of the teacher are done in between his subject, not because of it; his greatest works, thousands of them every week, are manifested as tiny incidences: a smile; a word; a private and unspoken understanding between teacher and pupil, invisible to all who do not know and feel the rich humanity of the classroom. These momentous works cannot be counted or measured, and let us be grateful for that. Nor can they be easily described to others without the describer sounding crass or vain. No, it is better to stay silent and enjoy what is, after all, the great perk of teaching.

I mentioned at the beginning of this chapter that I would attempt to offer some advice to the teacher in the field of practical discipline, as the natural complement to my discourse on the theory; this I am naturally reticent to do, since the reader may misunderstand my advice to be infallible. But may I remind the reader that we do not here pretend to be foolproof, we are merely making an attempt upon it; for though nothing works all of the time, if we attempt to make things foolproof we will get a better kind of fool. Furthermore, the advice that follows has been chosen so that even if it should fail to work, as all things in schools invariably will at some point, it will do so harmlessly, unless the teacher be at great pains to act in a particularly incompetent manner.

Refer all flatulence to the toilet

The scholar who deliberately breaks wind in class should be made to sign The Toilet Book and then promptly sent to the toilet, even though he will protest vehemently that he has no need of it. The reason for his being so reluctant to go is that such action singles him out as being unclean for society, and also because being ordered to the toilet by an adult is something that happens to six-year-olds.

When Mr Hills performed a flatus in my lesson, reflecting as much credit upon the contents of his diet as it did upon the unwholesomeness of his manners, two whole rows ran from their seats. He was clearly delighted with the mayhem he had caused, and presumably thought that as he was merely exercising a bodily function he was acting under some kind of biological immunity. I sent him to work in the toilet. When I looked down the corridor and saw him completing his work on the floor outside the toilet door, however, I took no small amount of satisfaction in noting that even he did not, in his more private moments, so savour the smell of human excrement.

I shared my flatulence protocols with a colleague who, as a mark of his great pedagogical foresight, has since sent to the toilet a boy who produced a foul-sounding noise from his armpit.

Two boys are half a boy

Immediately relieve from duty any scholar who, having been secured to perform an errand, asks if a friend can accompany him in the task. His longing for companionship betrays a lack of commitment to the task, and a tendency towards ease and misadventure. It is not for nothing that farmers of yesteryear were wont to make the unusual mathematical observation: one boy is a boy, two boys is half a boy and three boys is no boy at all.

Never admit to your own name

The teacher should never tell a child his age or first name, no matter how little a public knowledge of such details bothers him. Certainly, the scholars will find out such things easily enough – all that matters is that the information does not come from him. He might consider his name and age to be inconsequential trivia, but these seemingly insignificant details represent his private life, and a careful and affected guarding of them is a gentle reminder to the scholar that there are parts of the teacher's life that are not on offer. How many times I have insisted that I was christened Mister, or Sir, or told them that I was a foundling and have never known my age? Have I not, in the same week: claimed an age in five different decades; held at one time five wives, and been a bachelor; claimed, as my given name, every unlikely word beginning with J from Juandice to Jalapeño, from Jalopy to Jackanapés?

And did I not, upon phoning a mother, once hear the words, 'Oh, hello, you must be Jerusalem?' And did I not keep all those young scholars in happy beguilement, and at a safe distance too?

A person in authority ought to maintain a sense of privacy if he hopes to maintain that authority. Five-time world darts champion Eric Bristow maintained a mystique that made him unbeatable. Asked why he wasn't staying in a hotel with the rest of his English team-mates when representing his country, he replied, 'The day they know everything about me is the day they'll be me.' This wise cockney understood the need to keep secrets, and the meaning of the sign in the foyer of the Spy Museum, Tampere, Finland, which reads, 'Knowledge is power, secrets are hegemony.'

The teacher that precipitates celebrity status by furnishing children with all aspects of his identity encourages the idea that he is public property, and since (as I have noticed in my use of municipal lavatories) public property is not always used with kindness, the teacher would be well advised to deflect all enquiries into his private life.

Let me illuminate. The single teacher, if he be asked if he have a girlfriend – or she a boyfriend – would be well advised to inform the interrogator that he has trespassed onto business which is not his own; for if the teacher replies that he does not have a girlfriend, does he not invite the further question, 'Have you got a boyfriend,

Sir?' Now, whereas in the wider world such an enquiry might be genuine enough, in schools, say what you will, it is most commonly used with pejorative implications; and so 'Have you got a boyfriend, Sir?' can be deciphered as, 'I am calling you a homo, Sir, in front of the whole class, Sir – your move, Sir.' And if the teacher protests at the second question, his interviewer will counter with: 'There's nothing wrong with being gay, Sir – unless you're homophobic, Sir?' The teacher would be well advised not, at this point, to seek to prove his possible heterosexuality through a rehearsal of past events, for to do so would very likely culminate in an interview with the head. If the adversary is an experienced cor-ruptor of gravity then it matters not which way the teacher counters, for this is an exchange that he loses the moment he decides to jump two-footed into the clumsy and scarcely camouflaged trap.

Machiavelli's stratagem for the implementation of unpopular policies

For the first lesson with new classes in September the teacher should let everybody choose his own seat. Then, to the sound of the correct amount of grumbling, and for reasons which are both plentiful and obvious, he should swap the whole of the back row for the whole of the front row. Even if he feels that he does not need to move anybody, he may wish to do so anyway; for such an undertaking is a formidable display of might that cannot be repeated with the same theatre for another twelve months.

When implementing unpopular policies in his arrangements for the year ahead, such as the one just mentioned, the teacher should employ 'Machiavelli's stratagem for the implementation of unpopular policies' in order to reduce reciprocal resentment throughout the year.

> So it should be noted that when he seizes a state the new ruler must determine all the injuries that he will need to inflict. He must inflict them once for all, and not have to renew them every day, and in that way he will be able to set men's minds at rest and win them over to him when he confers benefits. Whoever acts otherwise, either through timidity or misjudgement, is always forced to have the knife ready in his hand and he can never depend on his subjects because they, suffering fresh and continuous violence, can never feel secure with regard to him. Violence must be inflicted once for all; people will then forget what it tastes like and so be less resentful.
>
> **Niccolò Machiavelli,** *The Prince*

The one-time wicked character that begins to exude good qualities is loved far more than the character that has always been good; but the softy who suddenly decides to employ uncharacteristic hardness is, on the off-chance that he is not openly mocked, remembered by his later violence, and not his former softness.

> Fool: Cry to it, nuncle, as the cockney did to the eels when
> she put 'em i' the paste alive. She knapped 'em o' the
> coxcombs with a stick and cried 'Down, wantons, down!'

William Shakespeare, *King Lear*

In this Shakespearean parable there lies a simple yet pro-
found message. The cockney wench tries to show kindness
to the eels by putting them into the pastry alive; not wishing
to bring about their inevitable death with a violent blow,
she hopes that the eels will die a more gentle death in the
oven. The eels, however, have other ideas, and the cockney
has to beat them violently over their heads with a stick
in order to put down the ensuing coup. By scanting her
proper duties she ends up having to be excessively brutal
– the very reverse of the kindness that she had originally
intended.

> I learned that it is the weak who are cruel, and that
> gentleness is to be expected only from the strong.

Leo Rosten, quoted in Leo Buscaglia,
Living, Loving and Learning

Interestingly, her self-inflicted sense of violation also precipitates a second measure of condemnatory censure, this
time delivered by that most malicious of weapons, the
tongue: 'Down, wantons, down,' she cries. This, too, is
a clear reversal of the naïve kindness that she had first
intended. Some children, like so many eels, are incapable
of appreciating acts of human kindness, and even when

the number of those who can is in the great majority, that majority will still provide the teacher with scant consolation; for he will be too busily employed in the knapping of the minority who cannot.

The teacher ought not to expect children to act like reasonable people: most invariably will, but the phenomenon should still be viewed from a position of surprise – a felicitous deviation from the norm, and policy should never be founded on such an uncertain premise. We must remind ourselves that discipline in schools is not designed with well-behaving scholars in mind; like the law, it is designed to thwart the few and protect the many. Some children even regard acts of kindness as a sign of weakness from teachers who lack conviction and confidence. I am firmly of the opinion that some of the bleakest moments in teaching come from having one's kindness mocked and returned.

The affectation of phlegm
If we could reckon the various deterrent powers of all of history's most grizzly forms of torture and capital punishment, and compare them to the deterrent qualities of a carefully affected incidence of phlegm, surely we would find that the latter has been a greater force in the prevention of wickedness than has the combined force of all of the former.

The diligent teacher will regularly apply, in the first instance, to an affectation of phlegm when seeking to restore order, or when he is desirous of order not being lost in the first instance. While a gentle phonetic rendering of 'Huck-hum' might satisfy his need in the last instance, an affectation of a protracted wrestle with a particularly stubborn piece of mucus will be required if he entertains hopes of bringing to order a classroom in high tumult. Such a silence achieved is worth ten silences got through a teacher's traditional recourse to mere volume.

Through my long and occasionally distinguished career as a schoolmaster I had intermittently made use of affected phlegm to chasten and subdue, but it wasn't until I encountered its use in literature (I know not where) that I developed a deeper confidence in the power of such a small undertaking. Suddenly I found myself on solid ground, walking in the secure knowledge that I was faux coughing where great men of education had faux coughed before me. I began to incorporate subliminal messages into my affected phlegms, giving issue to stray sentiments such

'Is that genuine phlegm, Sir, or affected?'

as 'scrawl', 'detention' and 'phone home', quickly moving onto elaborate intimations of breath-taking complexity. No eye contact, nothing clearly stated, just an underlying menace, a subtly coughed suggestion of behaviour that needed to be mended.

Phlegm affected even when nothing is amiss encourages the scholar in the belief that his teacher is able to see and hear evils that he himself is not even sensible of. Here we are at the heart of the matter, for to affect phlegm is to promote fear and deter wickedness.

Coming hither and going hence

The teacher must ensure that scholars do not enter and exit his room in an idiotic and chaotic fashion; for the natural progression from such a start can lead only to his misery. I will now offer the teacher a superior system by which to attempt to admit children into his classroom: boys line up one side of your door, girls the other – no bunching. Warm, polite and sincere greetings are exchanged. Children are referred to by name.

'Ladies, please go in.' (A nice variation here is for the boy at the head of the line to open the door.)

'Gentlemen, thank you.' (Appropriate hand gesture.)

The teacher goes in last (as the host this is only proper), thanking the boy who held the door open. Then ensues the taking off of coats and the unpacking of bags, all children upstanding behind their chairs. All uniform discrepancies need to be corrected, explained or excused at this point at the very latest, and ideally should not have been allowed over the threshold unchallenged. Wait for all parties to be unpacked and quiet.

'Ladies, please take a seat.'

'Gentlemen, please be seated.'

It is quite correct to be less formal with older children, particularly where they have opted to take your subject.

And so it must also be at the passing out: several minutes *before* the bells are due to sound, invite all to pack away and stand behind chairs. While waiting for the bells you may wish to say something wise or fascinating, or you may wish for the children to converse sophisticatedly – it is not necessary for them to wait in silence. The sounding of the bell will signal the requirement for quiet; a drawing pin will be raised, and a trustworthy child towards the rear of the room will confirm that a pin could be heard to drop onto the floor. Then invite, with fond farewells and appropriate gesticulation, the 'ladies' to leave; the 'gentlemen' follow in noble pursuit.

The marking of time

And the scribes and the Pharisees brought unto him a woman taken in adultery: and when they had set her in the midst, they say unto him, Master, this woman was taken in adultery, in the very act. Now Moses in the law commanded us that such should be stoned: but what sayest thou? This they said, tempting him, that they might have to accuse him. But Jesus stooped down, and with his finger wrote on the ground, as though he heard them not. So when they continued asking him, he lifted up himself, and said unto them, He who is without sin among you, let him first cast a stone at her.

John 8:3–7

Putting to one side the profundity of the response, I would like to draw the teacher's attention to what might be discovered in the seemingly insignificant act of writing in the sand. The hint that it is significant lies in the fact that it is even mentioned at all, for the Bible is not an unnecessarily descriptive book. That the writer does not tell us what was written inclines me to believe that what was written was not important. It has been suggested that Jesus was simply marking time when faced with a difficult problem, and perhaps the advice here is for us to do likewise.

If the teacher can resist the temptation to blurt out the first thing that comes into his head when he encounters adversity, he has a far better chance of coming up with a wise response – that is, one of the correct responses for the occasion, and not simply the one that satisfies his wrath. The pregnant pause also creates a heightened sense of tension into which the more considered response will a have greater impact. The considered response, spoken into the shocked silence that often follows the outburst of the wayward scholar, affords the teacher the opportunity of appearing both wise and unflappable. Marking time allows the teacher vital thinking time, but it also intensifies the atmosphere into which the drama unfolds – a drama played out before a most demanding class of critics, whose reviews will be circulating within the hour.

I recently had dealings with a scholar whose contempt for the school precepts, and more particularly a very reasonable request from myself, was to him a great source of joy. Unsure of the best way to proceed, I took the very sensible precaution of at least not doing the wrong thing, which precaution I enacted through writing things of no particular consequence on a piece of paper. This marking of time, it proved, worked to my ultimate advantage, for that night an inability to sleep caused me to devote more thought to the great event of the day, leading me to proceed with the matter thus:

Dear Mrs Hawkins,

I recently took the precaution of reminding everybody in my tutor group of some specifics regarding the school uniform code, as set out on p.22 of the pupil organiser. As I broached the notoriously treacherous area of footwear, and the stipulation of black shoes in place of the oft-favoured black trainer, I was heckled by your son, who informed me, in the roundest terms possible, that if I wanted him to wear black shoes then I would have to buy them for him myself.

Naturally, I was both incensed and injured by this very public slight on my discipline, but, the hour of wrath having passed, I begin to see that the suggestion is not without merit. To be short, Mrs Hawkins, I wish to take Gavin up in his offer. I understand that seeing Gavin properly shod will cost me deep in the purse; but I believe him to have been sincere in his offer, and a boy who can so readily estimate the solutions to his own problems should not be denied the means to realise those solutions, even though it should impinge on the pecuniary affairs of another.

I hope you will not think me forward if I suggest a Saturday for the shopping trip, with Truro as the preferred destination. From my own teenage remembrances of such expeditions I cannot think that the shoe buying would take any longer than four hours – five at the most; and if I were to pick him up at half-past-eight in the morning I could have him back to you by early in the afternoon, certainly no later than four.

I will contact you again in order to arrange a date, but must in the meantime congratulate you on the raising of a son who, though sometimes undiplomatic in his manner, has a conscience that wishes to do the right thing.

Yours sincerely,
Mr J. Andrews, Form Tutor

The 'Follow me!'

Sometimes a situation arises that will not allow for a night of contemplation, and the time marked does not provide the teacher with a clear way forward.

'Right, follow me!'

In the ensuing carry-on it is traditional to lead the wayward scholar up and straight back down a set of stairs, perform an unnecessary circuit, and expect the scholar to execute at least one emergency stop. Eccentric perambulatory flourishes are to be encouraged, particularly should you be fortunate enough to chance upon the scholar's close friends. Your itinerary should take you ominously close to the office of at least one senior teacher and, if it is seen to be empty, you may wish to knock on the door purposefully.

Refrain, as much as possible, from looking behind. To look behind – unless to address the scholar – is to betray doubt, and may well furnish he that follows with all the incentive required to attempt a straying.

When a suitable distance has been covered, the 'Follow me!' is ended, somewhat predictably, with the words 'WILL YOU STOP FOLLOWING ME!'

What to call children
After many years of deep contemplation on the matter may I suggest that when addressing children in their congregated form, the appellation 'ladies and gentlemen' is to be preferred above all others. 'You lot' implies, and thus encourages, a disorganised mass; 'Year 8', as in 'Right, Year 8', is dull and betrays the impersonal teacher who processes year groups and has little interest in the individual; the same can be said of timetable abbreviations such as 7 G2. 'Boys and girls' and 'children' – as in 'Now then,

children' – are far too babyish for secondary schools. Most importantly, however, the teacher must not ever use the word 'guys', except when referring to more than one bonfire effigy. 'Guys' – as in 'Right, guys' and 'OK, guys' – is an odious term understood by discerning children to issue from a fawning and sickly attempt by a teacher to come across as laid back and cool. It is also an Americanism, and as such should be left to Americans.

'Right, guys, listen up.'
'Oh no! Sir's desperate for our approval.'

I did once have the pleasure of working with a stunningly attractive mistress of divinity who was able to deliver a 'Boys, boys, boys' with such classy and sexual condescension that silly young male scholars could not help but oblige her. But hers was a particular talent, and I mention it for your reading pleasure only. For the rest of us, 'ladies and gentlemen' is the correct nomenclature. 'ladies and gentlemen' is the only epithet that is neither bland nor negative, and which actually has positive connotations built into it. 'Ladies and gentlemen' implies an expectation of behavioural decency, and has at least the potential, if nothing more, to encourage civilised behaviour.

> He always addressed us as 'gentlemen' and the possibility
> of behaving otherwise seemed thus to be ruled out from the
> beginning.
>
> **C.S. Lewis,** *Surprised By Joy*

Hasty ripostes, such as 'I ain't no lady', will need to be corrected both biologically and grammatically.

The discipline of names

The teacher must endeavour to learn as many names as he can, and to make use of them at every available opportunity. The teacher must not restrict himself to the names of those he teaches, or has taught, or to the names of popular or troublesome scholars – for do not all teachers know these names? No, he will find that the children use him much more kindly than some of his colleagues (for children gauge discipline by comparison, rather than outright reckoning) if he learns the names of the quiet and hitherto unknown children, both in his class and around the school. By attending to the first he wins allies in the mobile majority, whose allegiance is ever out to tender, and by attending to the second he guards against the fleeing of the scene, which, if accomplished with anonymity intact, often brings with it escape from all further consequences.

Of the two examples that now follow, one is the case of a boy who understood himself to be anonymous, but who was mistaken in this understanding; the other is that of a boy who, quite correctly, understood himself to be unidentifiable, but who did not manage to meet the first condition of anonymity, the successful fleeing of the scene.

I must respond to my name.
I must respond to my name.
I must respond to my name.
I must respond to my name.

I must not cover in cupboards
I must not cover in cupboards
I must not cover in cupboards
I must not cover in cupboards

The teacher who wishes to invest in his disciplinary reputation will go so far as to practise the names of his scholars through the use of lists and group photos; for, as already noted, the free and ready use of a schoolboy's name is a powerful tool in the winning of his allegiance.

If the reader should want further confirmation of this, he should covertly find out the names of four or five children whom he has never taught, or even spoken to. Then, quite naturally, he should greet them by name and observe their separate reactions.

> It is astonishing how sensible they are to notice from their betters, or those whom they think such. I do not speak of money, or gifts, or praise, or the more coarse and common briberies – they are more delicate courtiers; a word, a nod, a smile, or the mere calling of them by their names, is enough to ensure their hearts and their services.

> **Mary Mitford**, *Our Village*

I once worked under a headteacher who freely made it known that seven weeks into the new school year one of the first-years asked him what he did – a headteacher, mark you! At the other end of the spectrum a friend recounted to me how, when he was at school, a new headmaster took up his post while the students were away on their summer holidays. On Black Monday early in September, my friend, to his utter astonishment, was greeted by name by the new headmaster, whom he had never even seen before. The new headmaster had, it transpired, given over a portion of his summer holiday to studying form photos, and although it is most improbable that he could have named every child in this way, its selected application clearly had an effect, the playground ripples of which would have been felt by every child in the school. One headteacher had clearly made a very limited impression, even by the end of October, the other, with something as simple as a name wisely used, made an impression that long outlasted its intended purpose.

> I once interviewed Jim Farley and asked him the secret of his success. He said, 'Hard work,' and I said, 'Don't be funny.'
>
> He then asked me what I thought was the reason for his success. I replied: 'I understand you can call ten thousand people by their first names.'
>
> 'No. You are wrong,' he said. 'I can call fifty thousand people by their first names.'
>
> **Dale Carnegie,** *How to Win Friends and Influence People*

Being about to introduce myself to a new class in an unfamiliar school, I took the precaution of asking their previous teacher, a Mrs Fraser, for the names of those from whom I might expect some kind of try-out. She favoured me with two or three names – it is a pretty poor class that cannot give you two or three names – and I, through a feigned incompetence at getting the register filled in, acquainted myself with each of their faces. Some few minutes into my introduction a comedy sound was heard to come from my left – impossible to spell or describe in words, but redolent of the works of Benny Hill. With little to lose and much to gain I took a chance: 'I take it that was you, Mr Roberts, a most unfortunate hobby of yours, I believe?' The disbelieving faces of that scholar and his classmates was more precious reward than I could ever have dared to hope for. Not only had I survived the try-out of their champion, I had turned it to my advantage by performing favourably in front of the mobile majority; and it took nothing more than a name, and a modicum of good fortune.

The more names that a teacher is perceived to know, the more powerful he is perceived to be. A lot of bad behaviour in schools goes undisciplined due to the anonymity of the perpetrator: 'You boy, come back here!' is, to the wayward scholar, little more than an inducement to fly the boar before the boar pursues. This holds for the wider community as well as the school. I am convinced that if more teachers lived within their school catchments, rather than outside them, as is more typically the case, there would be far less antisocial behaviour, simply because the increased likelihood of identification would act as a deterrent to potential misdemeanants.

Never demand an apology

The teacher should never demand an apology. An apology that has to be forcibly extracted is not worth the having, and the act of having to ask for one is most unseemly. With all genuine apologies must come a genuine desire to act differently in the future, and it is not within the teacher's power to elicit such a desire. I am not saying that the teacher should not point out the appropriateness of an apology, merely that it is pointless for him to insist on one just for the sake of form: justice one can and should exact, but a repentant spirit is not ours to demand. This is not to say, however, that it may not be right and proper for a senior colleague to order an apology be given to the teacher, and for such an apology to be heard and accepted with all due ceremony – for this is the proper way for a school to run its apology policy. But when the teacher operates alone he should consider making use of lines in preference to the empty words of a forced apology; for lines represent the administration of justice, and may help the wayward scholar better to understand the error of his ways.

> I often get into troble because
> I seat near chris and he
> gets me into troble
>
> I often get into troble because
> I seat near chris and he
> gets me into troble

Lines are particularly good at dealing with low-level incidences of insolence and stupidity, such as: wilful and/ or gleeful flatulence; the making of woodland noises; hiding; falling over on purpose. Although usually met with the correct amount of grumbling, many wayward scholars grudgingly approve of being given lines because they are a badge of honour in the war against rules and adults. In parting from this topic I will add only that lines ought to embody the good-natured struggle between teacher and pupil, and, if likely to cause deep and lasting resentment, they should be avoided. Discipline, wherever possible, should be fun, both for he who gives and for he who receives; but when this delicate balance cannot be easily managed, it is he who gives that should be indulged.

The Pencils of Justice

Mr Richards of my tutor group sought an audience with me during which he delivered a complaint against Mr Wylde, a young scholar with whom he had lately been at odds. The accused, when cross-examined, complained that he had suffered severe provocation from Mr Richards, and stressed that the blows visited by him upon Mr Richards

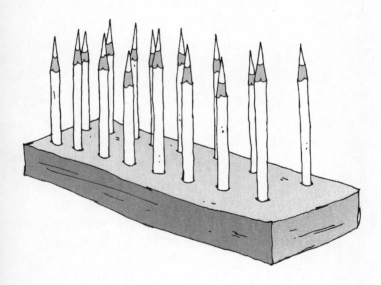

were simply his attempts at achieving parity. Being thus at considerable pains to apportion the proper amounts of blame and punishment, I sent for The Pencils of Justice.

Two pencils were immediately awarded to each boy for having contrived to bring contention into my life. Further examination soon revealed that every one of the thumps visited on the arm of the aggrieved party had been provoked by an annoying but utterly painless poke by the aggrieved party. The true reason for Mr Richards's complaint transpired to be not that he had been struck, but that his feeble pokes should have been exchanged for lusty blows, and for this alone he appealed to the law. I awarded him three pencils for the stupidity of having entered into a transaction wherein he received heavy blows for soft ones, while apparently making no attempt to renegotiate terms. A third boy was awarded two pencils for taking sides in a conflict in which he had not declared a formal interest. Further pencils were awarded for: Changing of the Story – which is a euphemism for lying; Hesitation – which is to slow the course of justice; and Withholding Vital Information – which is wilfully to waste my precious lunchtime. And so a verdict was arrived at by The Pencils of Justice.

I was 9/10 ths to blame for a TAT for tit incident
I was 9/10 ths to blame for a TAT for tit incident
I was 9/10 ths to blame for a TAT for tit incident
I was 9/10 ths to blame for a TAT for tit incident

Classroom types

It will be of enormous benefit to the teacher if he makes an attempt to identify classroom types: forewarned is forearmed. Below I offer the beginning of a list to which he will need to add, according to his own misfortune.

1. The Scapegoat
2. The Instigator
3. The Relief Instigator
4. The Occasional Trier
5. The Canned Laughter
6. The Grass
7. The Quibbler
8. The Fool
9. The Time Thief

Avoid ambiguity

The teacher must avoid ambiguity in what he asks for. There is a limited number of times that the teacher can say, 'Mr Lynch, turn around, please' (meaning, of course, face the front) before he encounters a Mr Lynch who will stand up, perform a pirouette, and then sit back down with a look of smug immunity. This cannot happen with, 'Face the front, please.'

Why is Miss Hastings standing in the bin? Miss Hastings is standing in the bin because her teacher, in a casual attempt to see her chewing gum put in its proper place, has said, 'Georgina – bin!' These are instances of poor-quality foolishness, and yet it is the teacher who is to blame, because he makes no attempt to be foolproof. And only this week did an outraged mistress of divinity complain to me that her stern reproof, 'I'm talking!' was met with 'So am I.'

The teacher must also avoid making a question out of an instruction. If he wants somebody to sit down, then he must tell him to, not ask him whether he will or won't. 'John, sit down, please' is a far better attempt at that which is foolproof than 'John, could you sit down, please?' While the latter will get him a blithe response from the kind of scholar who is experienced at not being in his seat, the former, because it is not a question, is far more difficult to debase.

The wayward scholar loves ambiguity in his teachers because it gives him licence to answer back, either in word or deed. With any luck he will get his teacher into a *contretemps* where he will stammer, mispronounce something or use the wrong word, offering, perhaps, an opportunity whereby the teacher might be more openly ridiculed. The wayward scholar loves to argue over non-mattering things, so I offer the reader the following piece of advice: never argue with an idiot, he will get you down to his level and then beat you on experience.

Crime and punishment

Wherever possible, attempt to make the punishment a perverse exaggeration or burlesque of the offence; for lessons in discipline are best learned when the consequence in some way resembles the crime. This being foremost in my thoughts, I decided to be creative with six children from my form referred to me for 'throwing white pencils around your classroom' – the very Pencils of Justice, mark you!

I first needed to establish levels of involvement in the orgy of chucking, so I invited the rest of the tutor group to vote on the level of involvement of each miscreant – low, medium or high. It was quickly to be seen through the show of hands that two of them had been lightly involved, one moderately and three highly. I then indulged them all in their love of pencil-throwing by having them stand in a circle in front of the class, throwing (passing is a more accurate description) a single white pencil round and round for a length of time proportional to the level of their involvement, but lasting not less than ten minutes. To guard against the encouragement of white-pencil throwing I would at intervals cry 'Change.' Upon this cry the direction in which the pencil was being thrown was reversed, so that the white pencil was both thrown and un-thrown. It is a wonderful thing to compel the wayward scholar to do something which, when illicit, is immensely fun, but when made compulsory, and in his own time, merely foolish and rather unfortunate.

Another such case concerned a Mr Ross, referred to me by his fellow scholars for striking a number of them on the head with a plastic bottle – a number that included young ladies. Clearly it was imperative that I knew precisely how hard these blows had been delivered, and so I invited – splendid word – Mr Ross to demonstrate this by striking himself on the head with the same weapon, which I was fortunate to discover in a bin near my classroom. Now, the reader will hardly credit the difficulty that those half dozen victims encountered in reaching a consensus as to the strength of the blows that they had suffered, and will be amazed to learn that Mr Ross must have beat himself about the head with the truncheon some thirty or forty times before agreement was reached, and before I could even begin to consider his punishment.

Similarly, when 12 children do not do their homework, it is clear that I am an object of ridicule: 'You have made me grievously unhappy today,' I declare at the beginning of their lunchtime detention, 'and because of this, you may not leave this room until you have made me laugh.' A short discussion ensued before their spokesperson approached my desk and announced, 'We are going to perform a homework play for you, Sir.'

Some haphazard rehearsals took place, and I fetched some other teachers to watch the performance with me. It was typically violent, and all those for whom a proper part could not be found died wanton and summary deaths. The high-point was a boy, playing my part, picking up the telephone and saying, 'Hello, Homework Grim Reaper, I've got 12 more for you.' It was a highly enjoyable detention, and one which all parties were sorry to see come to an end.

The two-minute detention

It is not the severity or particular nature of a sanction that determines its effectiveness, but the consistency with which it is applied, the suitability of the penalty, and its proximity in time to the offence. The greater the amount of time allowed to elapse between the incident and the action, the less the scholar will associate the two.

With the above in mind, let us consider the two-minute detention; for even the boy with a busy detention schedule will be hard pressed to deny his teacher two minutes at some point in the day. Two quality minutes of quiet reflection, with folded arms, will often serve just as well as would a whole lunchtime, for it is the inconvenience of a detention that is more troublesome to the scholar than its length. Most detentions are relatively easy to bear, once attended, but it is the pains which he is put to – parting with his friends; getting to the appointed place; taking his lunch alone; spending the best part of his lunchtime slightly out of kilter with his friends – that hurt him more sorely than the teacher might think.

A detention of two minutes' length also sympathises with the idea that one should never leave a child with nothing: for while there is still the majority of a breaktime to lose, there remains an incentive for the scholar to steady his behaviour; if the whole breaktime is already lost, he acts under sound economic principles if he gets full and wicked value for that which is already irretrievable. The teacher loses much of his power to negotiate for improved behaviour when he tells the wayward scholar to expect no break at all. Even the teacher who threatens bulk detentions, encouraging the scholar in the belief that much can still be lost, tacitly acknowledges the disciplinary impotence of his detentions in general: the problem that cannot be solved by one detention is unlikely to be solved by two, or even three. Furthermore, *that* teacher will pay for his excesses with all of the work attendant upon detentions that run into next week. And what is a detention next week – or even tomorrow? In the simple and impulsive mind of the wayward scholar it hardly exists at all.

In addition, the two-minute detention is easy to manage, and so the teacher's threat can always be delivered: there is, after all, nothing more corrosive to good discipline than empty-threat-making, which habit is significantly more harmful to the teacher and his authority than his deployment of a Nelsonian eye. If happenings confirm two minutes to be insufficient, the teacher still has full recourse to the more traditional lengths of detainment, and nothing has been lost.

Walk awhile

The teacher should never attempt to reason with a difficult child – and it is certainly possible for him to do that – in front of the rest of his class. He should endeavour to talk through his differences with the truculent scholar while taking a gentle stroll around the school with him, or by discussing the matter while they both lean over a railing. Not only do such contingencies remove them both from the source of most problems, the classroom, it also places them side-by-side instead of head-to-head. Away from the madding crowd they will both have a greater chance of being reasonable. Walking and gazing have a hypnotising effect, and differences do not seem quite so insurmountable when you are taking a gentle stroll together in the same direction.

Toss for it

You don't get any straight answers out of a boy, so when dealing with a dispute between two unreliable parties the teacher may wish to toss a coin to see who is first to give his uninterrupted version of events. Having heard both sides of the story in their entirety the teacher will then be in a better position to judge which version he considers to be the less unlikely of the two.

When two scholars from my form were referred to me for a violent dispute over personal property, and were unable to agree on a unified version of the truth, I found myself in the difficult position of having to punish both; let both off; or call one of the boys a liar and risk the attentions of an angry parent. In order to give me thinking time, I decided, with their help, to draw a diagram of the supposed events. We mainly drew things upon which unanimity could be reached, such as the position of the door, the teacher's desk, but most importantly where each boy was sitting. It was quickly evident that in order for the boys to have had an altercation over the contents of a pencil case, one boy would have needed to be out of his seat and across the room. As his story was the first to be exposed as being less than the total truth, he took the blame.

Write this down

Finally, in times of great tribulation, get them copying; for as a wise old man of education once advised me, 'Get their heads down: when they're copying, they're harmless.'

Epilogue

If we are going to have wayward scholars in our schools – and I think there is little enough doubt that we always will – then let us at least move for a better standard of waywardness; for though nothing works all of the time, if we try to make things foolproof, we will get a better quality of fool. And what is there that more readily exemplifies that ancient and honourable struggle 'twixt scholar and school than a fool of the better sort.

Let us not, though, put too much faith in method, or delight in the use of noxious strategies: for teaching ever was art over science. Yes, in the garden of education the weeds must be checked if the fruit is to be sweet, but let us attend to the matter with the probing and humane hoe rather than the pesticides of the intensive educationalist.

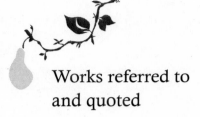

Works referred to
and quoted

with grateful thanks for permissions given

Henry B. Adams, *The Education of Henry Adams* (Houghton Mifflin Co., Boston and New York, 1918)

The Bible, King James version

James Boswell, *The Life of Samuel Johnson*, vol. I (1791)

E.R. Braithwaite, *To Sir, With Love* (Bodley Head, London, 1959)

R. Buckminster Fuller, *I Seem to Be a Verb: Environment and man's future* (Bantam Books, New York, 1970)

Leo F. Buscaglia, *Living, Loving and Learning* (Ballantine Books, New York, 1983)

Dale Carnegie, *How to Win Friends and Influence People* (Simon & Schuster, New York, 1936)

William Cobbett, *Advice to Young Men, and (Incidentally) to Young Women, in the Middle and Higher Ranks of Life* (1829)

R.F. Delderfield, *To Serve Them All My Days* (Hodder & Stoughton, London, 1972)

Henry Fielding, *Tom Jones* (1749)

John Garretson, *The School of Manners* (1701)

William Golding, *Lord of the Flies* (Faber & Faber, London, 1954)

Gilbert Highet, *The Art of Teaching* (Vintage Books, New York, 1989)

James Hilton, *Goodbye, Mr Chips* (Hodder & Stoughton, London, 1934)

Thomas Hughes, *Tom Brown's School Days* (1857)

Thomas Jefferson, Letter to James Madison (30 January 1787)

Jerome K. Jerome, *Three Men in a Boat* (1889)

Rudyard Kipling, *Stalky & Co.* (1889)

Robert Lacey and Danny Danziger, *The Year 1000: What life was like at the turn of the first millennium* (Little, Brown & Company, London, 1999)

C.S. Lewis, *Mere Christianity* (Macmillan, London, 1952)

C.S. Lewis, *Surprised By Joy* (Harvest Books, London, 1955)

Niccolò Machiavelli, *The Prince* (1532), translated by George Bull (Penguin Books, London, 1961)

Frank McCourt, *Teacher Man* (Harper Perennial, London, 2006)

Mary Mitford, *Our Village* (1835)

Miyamoto Musashi, *A Book of Five Rings* (1643), translated by Victor Harris (Allison & Busby, London, 1974)

George Orwell, *The Road to Wigan Pier* (Victor Gollancz, London, 1937)

George Orwell, 'Such, Such Were the Joys', in *Such, Such Were the Joys and Other Essays* (Harcourt, Brace, Jovanovich, New York, 1953)

Michael Rosen, 'I was Mucking About in Class', in *The Complete School Verse* (Red Fox, London, 1998)

Seneca, *On Tranquillity of Mind*, translated by C.D.N. Costa (Penguin Books, London, 1997)

William Shakespeare, *Hamlet* (1603)

William Shakespeare, *King Lear* (1608)

William Shakespeare, *The Merchant of Venice* (1600)

Muriel Spark, *The Prime of Miss Jean Brodie* (Macmillan, London, 1961)

Michael Twist, *The Spacious Days* (Farming Press, Ipswich, 1992)

Hugh Walpole, *Mr Perrin and Mr Traill* (Mills & Boon, London, 1911)

Evelyn Waugh, *Decline and Fall* (Chapman & Hall, London, 1928)

David Winkley, *Handsworth Revolution: The odyssey of a school* (Giles de la Mare, London, 2002), www.gilesdelamare.co.uk